Bringing Back The

WHITE
PINE

By Jack Rajala

⅄ TABLE OF CONTENTS ⅄

ISBN # 0-9662779-0-2

Printed in U.S.A. by Pro Print of Duluth, MN.

FORWARD: THE JUDGMENT

The question of what really happened to the vast forests of white pine that were once present in Minnesota, and who was responsible for the demise of those forests continues to be the subject of great debate. Of even greater contentious discussion is the question of what to do now to bring the white pine back.

Since my family's history and that of one of our sawmills span the time from the days of abundant white pine forests to the present, I recognize the need to take responsibility for what has happened to the great monarchs of the north woods. No sawmill has a longer history of harvesting this wonderful wood than the Rajala pine mill in Big Fork, a land where the river runs north.

Every year for almost 100 years now, white pine logs have been driven down the river, hauled by sleigh, or trucked into this northern mill site and then sawed into volumes of incredulous lumber and millwork products. But there have been other mills and generations of forest managers who have also played important roles in what happened to white pine. I accept only my share of the judgement for what resulted.

In her book, "The White Pine Industry in Minnesota," Agnes Larson referred to the *"voracious appetite for*

lumber of a fast growing country," (p. vii) and the mills—
small and large—that fed that appetite with white pine.
Gone are the big mills and the big names of the 19th
and early 20th century, but the demand for lumber still
remains and so does a new generation of lumbermen.
Again, referring to the days of the vast white pine cutting, Larson went on to say: *"For all this a price was paid.
One cannot with impunity rob Mother Nature of her treasures, for truly the sins of the fathers are avenged unto the
third or fourth generation. The price we must pay for the
rapid use of our forests is a vast area of wastelands for generations, or else a wise and vigorous policy of reforestation."*

When she wrote these words in 1945, little could she
know how long the avenging would last or how long it
would take for us to commence a major effort to bring
back white pine.

I hope that **"Bringing Back the White Pine"** helps to
put some context to this magnificent resource. I also
hope that, as a silvicultural reference, this book will
offer encouragement to others who, like I, are willing to
do what is necessary to ensure we will always have white
pine in our forests.

SECTION
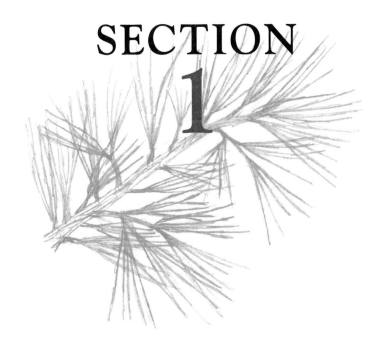
1

INTRODUCTION

INTRODUCTION

Many factors, in combination, have caused the decline of white pine—logging, land clearing, natural enemies, and forest policy (or lack of it). There is plenty of responsibility to go around. In the 1996 debate about imposing a legislative moratorium on any further harvesting of white pine as a way of saving this tree, blame for the species' demise centered around those of us who harvest some of these trees for the marvelous wood products that we make. The other "culprits" often blamed for the demise are the forest land managers; most often mentioned is the Minnesota Department of Natural Resources. Those of us who are blamed can shoulder the criticism.

Some believe the real issue is how do we *save* the white pine we have left. Placing a moratorium on any or all cutting of white pine will, admittedly, "temporarily" save some white pine trees. But unfortunately, those trees will all eventually succumb to natural enemies and the white pine will be essentially gone.

The critical issue really is restoration—What should we do to *bring back* white pine? How do we get pro-active in forest policy and practices to restore white pine again? Simply stated: The issue is regeneration, not preservation. The ultimate purpose of this handbook is to make a case for active management of white pine restoration through regeneration.

From a lifelong experience in milling this wonderful wood, we know that homeowners and woodworkers highly value white pine for its aesthetic and working qualities. As a native tree in the Minnesota landscape, we also know how critically important and valuable white pine is to the forest itself—a part of the mosaic of tree species that form the home for forest life; as super canopy towering above all else in its own exquisite majesty. It is little wonder that those who come to visit Minnesota's forests are most impressed by these majestic sentinels. It is assumed that white pine are the pillars of the forest. As such, this tree has no equal.

Foresters are cautious people who are steeped in the discipline of science and natural order. They know that growing white pine is difficult and expensive. The virtual elimination of periodic natural fires, deer browsing, and the introduction of blister rust during this century have changed the science and natural order of the forest. White pine will not "just happen" like it did 150 years ago. Today, regenerating and growing white pine requires a pro-active approach. If we want to bring it back, we have to do far more than wait for it to just happen—we have got to get out there and make it happen.

Twenty years ago we asked, 'Why doesn't the forestry community actively and aggressively promote white pine?' The answer was, 'It's too difficult.' This statement was often followed by a litany of scientific and economic rationale. However, some of us challenged reason; we were determined to try anyway—to just go do it.

Difficult? Yes! Growing white pine has been scientifically more challenging than we imagined and economically more expensive than we had ever planned. But the rationale for white pine has changed too. Forest landowners and the general public want to bring back white pine. The difficulty is only relative to what, and how much, we are willing to invest and how hard we are willing to work. The case for white pine has never been clearer—and it's a good one.

SECTION 2

A BRIEF HISTORY OF WHITE PINE

CHAPTER 1

A BRIEF HISTORY OF WHITE PINE

➢ Part I - Origin of Eastern White Pine

Thousands of years ago, before the last ice age, Minnesota had two basic forest types—the boreal forest in the north and a hardwood forest in the south. Researchers have determined that white pine did not exist in any abundance in the area prior to 7,000 years ago.

Interestingly, Minnesota is the very edge of the white pine range and much of what is left of this tree species, like those trees now seen at Itasca State Park, is at the very "edge" of the edge.

Prior to European settlement of North America, white pine was prominent both along the North Atlantic coast, throughout New England, and all the way along the Great Lakes region west into Minnesota. A common misconception is that white pine is native to the area and has always been here. *"Paleo-ecological evidence reveals that the distribution and abundance of white pine have varied greatly across northeastern North America during the past 12,000 years . . ."* (Jacobson, White Pine Symposium, p. 19)

Approximately seven centuries ago, white pine began its westward expansion from the Atlantic seaboard, but then ceased its movement for several thousand years. Experts have found that white pine began its most significant movement into greater Minnesota about 4,000 years ago after the passing of a period of warm, dry climate that had favored the growth of oak forests. It is also suggested that this expansion of white pine was probably in response to a lower frequency of fire associated with a cooler, more moist climate at the arid end of its range.

Like other tree species, the spread of white pine is closely associated with climatic change. Its presence today is remarkable, having probably survived the 40 or so quaternary ice ages *"only because the continental shelves off the mid-Atlantic Coast were not ice covered."* (Jacobson, White Pine Symposium Proceedings, p. 19) This suggests that the eastern seaboard is the origin of Eastern white pine. It also seems evident that the species followed the receding glaciers until it finally reached northern Minnesota.

Not only has the presence of white pine depended on climate, but it appears that its abundance has also been greatly affected by climate. *"Perhaps the most interesting and dramatic tie to climate change is the 4,000 year-long reduction of abundance of white pine that occurred prior to the timber harvesting era of the past century."* (Jacobson, White Pine Symposium, p. 22)

After a long time in coming, white pine spread out westward across Minnesota quite rapidly. Jacobson explains this movement: "*Beginning about 4,000 years ago, the prairie/forest border began to shift to the west and white pine followed. This final expansion was rapid, especially across the northern third of the state where a shift of more than 60 miles occurred in just 1,000 years (between 3,500 years before present (YBP) and 2,500 YBP.) Thereafter, changes continued somewhat more slowly until the time of logging. In fact, some of the major pine forests, and especially those of central Minnesota, had been present for only a few generations when they were cut for lumber.*" (Jacobson, White Pine Symposium, p. 22)

This all makes the saying, "virgin white pine," (a colloquialism that was often used to define why some white pine was more valuable to mills and markets) seem even more realistic than anyone originally knew.

The presence and abundance of white pine is closely related to climate although it is generally considered to be very site tolerant. Scientists believe that although the years of increase were drier and warmer than today, the species requires a moisture/temperature regime where precipitation equals evapo-transpiration. To confirm this, white pine's best days seem to have been when it fit clearly between a dry site, oak regime to its south and west, and the more moist and cool regime of the boreal forest to its north.

From a climatological point, its niche seems to be well defined. During the past 4,000 years, Minnesota's landscape and climate became home for the species. Because the state's landscape and climate are so varied, the amount of white pine from region to region also varied.

There are some who claim that at the time of early European settlement, the state had 3 -1/2 million acres of white pine of a total of over 30 million acres of all forest.

And, although there is evidence to show that much of the early white pine occurred as single trees or as a small component of other forest cover types, records and research also show that there were heavy concentrations of white pine in the east-central and north-central areas of the state.

🗡 Part II · Early Lumbering in Minnesota

Like so much of the history of Minnesota, the Mississippi River is at the center of the state's early lumbering history. When Jean Nicollet looked out over the broad reaches along the great river in 1634, he probably was the first white man to see the treasure of resources reaching back from its shores for miles and miles.

This "second greatest of all river valleys in the world" had fur, forests, and rich fertile land. Fur was the first to be capitalized upon. The explorers used the trapping skills of the native Americans and the renowned voyageurs transported the valuable pelts off to the East for shipment to Europe.

"But eventually the fur trade gave way to the lumber industry and, by 1850, fur no longer held first place. The region was then yielding the second greatest resource to be taken from its breasts. Lumber had become the dominant industry

both in Minnesota and in other parts of the Upper Valley".
(Agnes Larson, "History of the White Pine Industry in
Minnesota, 1949," pg. 4)

Just as it would appear that the fur trade opened the
door to the vast rivers and forests of Minnesota, it would
also appear that lumbering helped expose the land to
settlement and agriculture. Eventually much of the
"eternal forest" was laid down and the lands were settled
by the very men who worked in the camps, rode the log
drives, and bulled the lumber through the mills. Some
authors infer that these thousands of men were only
passing through to cut the pine. Granted, many of the
mill owners were entrepreneurs from Maine, Missouri,
and Michigan who later moved on west. But it is well-
known from present day family histories that most of the
manpower of the big logging era came for land, and settled down when the bulk of the timber was gone.

The first were probably English, Irish, Scots, and French
who indeed followed the timber. But the bulk of the
people were of German, Swedish, Norwegian, Finnish,
and Polish descent who had "old country" rural back-
grounds and were accustomed to painfully hard woods
work. They wanted land to settle. The immigrants were
to experience the golden age of lumbering in Minnesota
and eventually saw it come to an end. But in its day,
lumber was to make great changes in the entire region.

*"It created the capital so basic to the building of a new coun-
try and was to go in advance of wheat as it were . . . And
the chief lumber of the region was white pine, the Pinus
Strobus."* (Larson, p. 4)

JIM KASPER©

It is easy to imagine how enticing the harvest of the early pine was—virgin, abundant stands of stately trees, soft to cut, light in the water, and excellent to build with. The white pine of the upper Mississippi was a magnificent tree. What is hard to imagine today is whether the accounts that historian Agnes Larson used could be true: "(Trees) 200 feet tall, with 160 more normal." This would be hard to prove. But we can agree that some had a "diameter of four to five feet." Early pictures and records, however, indicate that two to three feet were the normal diameters of the original pine.

Other accounts made by Larson are equally interesting and informative: *The white pine grew in a variety of soils, but wherever it grew, moisture was necessary. It grew luxuriously in heavy clay and loam soils, where it intermingled with the hardwoods. The white pine grew best in a soil that had a mixture of sand. Far north on the steep rocky slopes of Lake Superior it grew with the spruce and the tamarack. The white pine grew in river bottoms where there was good drainage, or where the rainfall was heavy, averaging between 26 and 35 inches. It stopped abruptly within about forty miles of prairie country where the rainfall was less.*

"*No other soft wood had so many desirable qualities. It was strong, slow to decay, light in weight, odorless, and easy to cut, thus yielding readily to pattern work. It seasoned well and it had strong resistance to weather and time.*

"*No other softwood has served more usefully in America than has the white pine. Its abundance, cheapness, and varied usefulness made it an important factor in the westward movement. It furnished the early settler with shelter. The logs for the cabin, the shakes for the roof, and the puncheons for the floor all came from the white pine. It also provided the incoming settler with implements, furniture, fences—all of them necessities in a new country."* (Larson p. 5)

White pine was present throughout most of the wooded areas of what is now Minnesota when the first sawing began in 1839. But the finest pineries lay along the Mississippi starting at the junction with the St. Croix, and north to the Canadian border, according to the records that Larson found. She claimed that the best was east of the river and the very best was in the area of Carlton County.

"There was coniferous forest reaching from the east banks of the Mississippi to the boundary line of Canada. The tree that gave character and distinction to this whole region, which was larger than the state of Maine, was the white pine. This tree for at least five decades dominated the lumber industry in Minnesota. The section which lay nearest to the Mississippi and the region of the St. Croix was most prominently the home of the white pine." (Larson, p. 7)

It was fitting that these pineries should be close to major waterways, the St. Croix and the Mississippi, because the rivers would readily transport the buoyant white pine to the mills downstream. It is little wonder that the earliest log cutting was for mills in St. Louis and other mill towns down river. However, as early as March 13, 1837, Henry H. Sibley, Lyman M. Warren, and William A. Aitkin bargained with the Chippewa tribes for cutting rights on the St. Croix and Snake Rivers to be allowed to cut timber and erect mills. (Larson, p. 13) In 1838, the U.S. government bought much of the St. Croix lands from the Indians.

"The land thus purchased was the most remote part of the old Northwest Territory . . . The purchase by the U.S. government of the land in 1838 was the first step toward establishment of lumbering as a commercial enterprise in the last outpost of the white pine which had extended from Maine to Minnesota." (Larson, p. 14)

In 1839, L.S. Judd, David Hone, and Orange Walker built the first sawmill in Minnesota at Marine-on-St. Croix and, in 1844, the first sawmill in Stillwater began its steady hum. Within 10 years, five more mills were sawing at Stillwater.

Where were the markets for the pine lumber of these early days? Certainly not in Minnesota for it had a population of less than 5,000 in 1849, according to Larson's account. No, the markets were down the Mississippi: Dubuque, Clinton, and St. Louis. It was through these cities that the great influx of new Americans were passing to settle the great plains. It was the white pine, largely from Minnesota, that made it all possible. Just the logs passing through the Stillwater "boom" from 1840 to 1874 totaled over 3 1/2 billion board feet. (Larson p. 33)

It seems fitting that the entrepreneurs from St. Louis were the ones to profit from the earliest of the upper Mississippi and St. Croix white pine because they had been there to see the decline of the area's fur and had helped bring about the transition to timber.

The next era of harvesting white pine had a lot more to do with Minnesotans. And the next generation of lumbering had far less to do with exploitation than it had to do with pushing back the wilderness to make room for the on-rush of settlers being wooed to the Minnesota Territory. Agnes Larson commented that *"People came to St. Paul in such numbers that they could not be housed. Many of them had to camp in the streets until they could make proper arrangements. The 'advancing millions' were fast taking possession of the new territory."* (Larson, pps. 31-32)

To the lumber industry, this movement of population was of double consequence. Minnesota was beginning to produce its own food stuffs. Agriculture required clearing the land first, presumably. But even more important, the increasing population within the state opened a new market for the white pine of Minnesota.

Whereas the *first* chapter about white pine lumbering deals mostly with the St. Croix, the next was centered on the upper Mississippi. Here again, the action centered around a waterfall for power and a headland of good pine above. This time it was St. Anthony Falls, the present location of Minneapolis, and the pineries of the Rum River located only 40 miles upstream.

Franklin Steele was the foresightful man who saw the opportunity in lumbering, purchased the water power and mill site at St. Anthony, and started sawmilling white pine in 1848. Larson claims that Steele *"must have foreseen that Minneapolis would become a great market"* and that *"credit is due him for his stamina in holding on under difficulties that, at times, would have made a less resolute man give up."* Since much of the timber available to the mill belonged to the Indians, it is reported that the mill had to negotiate with Chief Hole-in-the-Day for timber to supply the mill. The astute old Indian demanded half a dollar for every white pine tree cut.

So convinced was Larson of what her research of these early times indicated that she said of Steele: *"Virtually he was the founder of Minneapolis."* If that is the case, then it only seems logical to conclude that Minneapolis was started as a sawmill town.

What happened during the next 50 to 60 years after these first beginnings of lumbering white pine in Minnesota will long be debated. Was the press of settlement with the tools of axe and saw inevitable? Or is this a dark spot in the history of Minnesota's fine forests and a calamity that had mostly to do with the ambitions of men and their affinity for profit? Looking back on this time, one could draw either or both conclusions. But from all accounts, at least the beginning of the white pine logging era seems legitimate, understandable, and acceptable as an important chapter in how Minnesota came to be.

The mass of white pine logs that flowed from upstream and from across the watersheds of the Mississippi, the St. Louis, and the rivers running north were almost incomprehensible to most of us today. This era hosted all the color and excitement of the lumberjack, the logging camp, oxen, horses, log drives, and railroads. This relatively short period of history changed the white pine forest eternally, orchestrated and carried out, first by men from Maine like Daniel Stanchfield and Ard Godfrey, and then later by the more familiar names of men like De Laittre and Bovey. They, in turn, were followed by entrepreneurs like John and George Pillsbury, John Laird, and Matthew Norton.

↗ Part III · By the Turn of the Century

Among the many wonders of the logging era in Minnesota history are the rates of advance and the reach demonstrated by this still-young industry. Without railroads or highways, the captains of white pine thrust rapidly further and further north and west, always following, of course, the rivers that were the key to success of this rapidly moving industry. The timber cruisers pressed on up the Mississippi to places like Little Falls, Brainerd, Aitkin, and Grand Rapids. The "great river" changes its mostly northern course at Brainerd, swings northeast and, in turn, swings back heavily west at Jacobson in the very northeast corner of Aitkin County. From there it traverses the breadth of Itasca, Cass, and Beltrami counties from its source in Clearwater County. By 1900, enormous amounts of white pine had been driven down the river from these vast headlands—a most novel fact of a truly novel industry.

Not to be forgotten in any history of lumbering in Minnesota, and especially that of white pine in northern Minnesota, is the fact that many of the "bigger than life" men of the log drives were Canadien. From the east came men of great ambition and entrepreneurial spirit.

One of these was a very young man who came from New Brunswick. At 18 years of age, Gulford G. Hartley came to make a start for himself, first coming to Brainerd and then on to Aitkin in 1872. Hiring on as a teamster, he was sent further north to Wabana Lake in Itasca County where he put in his first winter in the Minnesota woods.

The career of G.G. Hartley closely resembled the history of pine logging of the next 20 or so years. The unpublished family diary, "The Life and Times of G.G. Hartley" (1853-1922) includes a litany of items that help describe this white pine era in the environs from Brainerd to Bemidji, especially the stretch from Aitkin to Cass Lake:

1873 - "This cut by Day & Sons of Minneapolis were the first logs driven on the Prairie River . . . They had to be taken across Wabana Lake."

1874 - "They staked out their claims, built their cabins, and planned to buy stumpage on adjoining lands with such scrip as they could get."

1883 - "Built a dam on Bass Creek (where the village of Cohasset is now located) to supply water to drive our logs out the following spring" . . . "Cut was taken down to Brainerd, sawed by Ebner H. Bly and then sold to the Northern Pacific RR."

Americans and Canadiens alike, they were all foreigners to this new country of Minnesota, the land of the last of the white pine. Together, logging crews like the Hartleys pushed their supplies up every tributary of the Mississippi each fall. They spent the winter cutting from 1,000,000 board feet in the small camps to 10,000,000 board feet in the large camps during the winter months. In the spring they drove their logs down the Leech, the Prairie, the Swan, and all the other headland rivers to form the "big drive" going down the Mississippi.

Hard-pressed for mechanical power, they got every ounce of strength from the oxen, horses, and the men they employed. When one walks the same river drive paths that men like Hartley did, now over 100 years later, there is a sense of overwhelming awe at the fortitude and ingenuity these 19th century loggers exhibited. Think of it—over 120 years ago, Hartley took the big pine off the upper Prairie River which is so remote that years go by now without a single person going into some of these areas—areas that are still vast wilderness.

Authors note: Although Itasca Lumber Company (the Joyce family) took the white pine out of the Wolf Lake Camp area north of Grand Rapids and right at the south foot of the Laurentian Divide, Hartley set up camp there in the late 1890s so that he could fish and hunt with his early buddies, like John Greenway and Dan Gunn. Both here in the area around Wolf Lake Camp and at the confluence of the Clearwater River with the Prairie River, (this is the area where Hartley claims he buried Chief Wabana "below frost."), I can, to this day, feel the presence of this early logger and his compatriots.

The reason for the end of the 19th century white pine logging frenzy is commonly thought to be that 'all the pine was gone.' A look at "The Birth of a Forest," (an

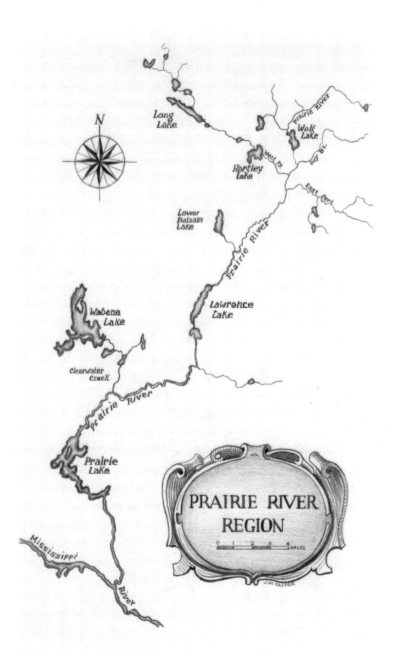

Long Lake

Prairie River

Wolf Lake

Hartley Lake

West Fk.

Day Bk.

East Fork

Lower Balsam Lake

Prairie River

Wabana Lake

Lawrence Lake

Clearwater Creek

Prairie River

Prairie Lake

Mississippi River

PRAIRIE RIVER REGION

0 1 2 3 4 MILES

JIM KASPER

account of the formation of the Chippewa National Forest 1898-1907) would say otherwise. Much of what was left of the timber was on government or Indian ceded land. Loggers got at the timber with the use of "scrip." Almost like legal tender, scrip could be negotiated and used as payment to the government. Some scrip was more authentic, such as the scrip given Civil War veterans. The scrip served like promissory notes that were redeemable to purchase federal land. Other scrip issued to Indians was also highly valued. Large blocks of timber stumpage were negotiated with scrip and much from making "less than always honorable deals" with the Indians.

In an attempt to curb abuses in timber stumpage dealings and also to start preserving some forest areas for the future, plans were laid to create a Minnesota forest reserve in 1901. This, in time, became the Chippewa National Forest; it is the oldest federal forest east of the Rocky Mountains. It was this change in government timber policy (ironically driven by women's clubs in Minneapolis) that stopped the big logging thrust. Hartley and many of the then-captains of the timber industry greatly resented the changed policies.

According to "The Birth of a Forest," extreme measures were taken to beat back the forest reserve policy. This source even suggests that severe stomach poisoning contracted by the first forest supervisor in 1905, could have been more than coincidental because "it was believed that he had been poisoned in the hotel in Cass Lake where he was stopping. It was owned by Hartley." (p. 12).

This was authored by none other than Gifford Pinchot who had taken personal responsibility to establish what was first known as the Minnesota National Forest (now the Chippewa). Certainly, a chapter in the era of white pine logging was about to come to an end.

⯈Part IV · The Last Hurrah

By 1910, sawmilling the white pine in Minnesota and the Lake States had lost most of its thrust. The major pineries had been cut hard and fast. The eternal forest was not as endless as some had thought and only pockets of land and remote areas had pine left.

The big sawmills on the St. Croix were gone and so were those at St. Anthony on the Mississippi. At St. Anthony the sawmills had been replaced by another institution—the flour mills. The money and the entrepreneurs had turned to a new resource—wheat—a resource that would last much longer because people were prepared to plant it with each new season after the harvest of the previous year. Agriculture, they understood; forestry, they did not.

All the water courses—the Mississippi, the Rum, the St. Croix, the Snake—showed the skeletons of an age gone by. Scattered, sunken, and dead-headed logs littered the sand bars, meadows, and lake and river bottoms. The rivers still ran with a head of icy spring runoff water each March, but there were no logs, no wannigans or batteaus. And certainly no "river pigs" were working the drives. An era had come to an end—almost.

From the turn of the century and into the early 1930s,

there was another transient time of glory for a few sawmillers. In 1910, Fredrick Weyerhaeuser made one last grand stand by building a huge mill at Virginia in northeastern Minnesota where thousands of sections of virgin forest remained. Paradoxically, he built as his final thrust in Minnesota the world record sawmill of the day. This course of history seems to say that Weyerhaeuser was in a hurry to finish up the job of cutting out the Minnesota pine in short order, for the mill cut up to a world record number of 1,000,000 board feet per day. Rarely, if ever, has this been done anywhere else. The Virginia and Rainy Lake Mill included a massive railroad system for logging; many of the old railroad grades are still very evident in northeastern Minnesota to this day.

The other "last hurrah" for the white pine industry was Edward Backus' huge operation at International Falls located on Minnesota's northern border. Probably no less than 20,000 sections of what was left of the northern Minnesota forest constituted the Backus forest domain. He, too, methodically laid out a web of railroads and drove the water courses—all to feed the huge sawmill at the lower end of Rainy Lake. Backus went bust during the Great Depression of the 1930s. Even his seemingly indomitable spirit gave up when he found himself in the position of desperately seeking new capital, and embroiled in a debate with early preservationists over issues of river dams and water levels.

The forest has a way of hiding some of its treasures, and it has an amazing ability to follow a successional cycle to

renew itself. For even after having supplied world record amounts of pine for almost 100 years—70 years in the south, 30 in the north—there has always been a remnant left. And it's this remnant that has supplied the smaller sawmills of this era for now almost another 70 years.

The Hedstrom Mill at Grand Marais, operating since 1915, and the Rajala Mill in Big Fork, since 1902, have sawn white pine every year and never missed a cut. As though waiting for a new white pine era to dawn, these operations continue to make smaller amounts of world class white pine lumber, while living mostly on aspen, spruce, and the supposed replacement for white pine—red pine.

SECTION
3

WHY GROW WHITE PINE?

TABLE 1   PINE SAWTIMBER SOLD

CHAPTER 2

WHY GROW WHITE PINE?

In earlier chapters it was mentioned that Minnesotans love white pine. On the one hand, these majestic pines are silhouettes that harken back to an earlier age—a time before man "spoiled" things—an almost mythical sense of the natural world. The white pine are the great sentinels that connect us to that time.

On the other hand, white pine represents our hope for forests of the future. Today there is tremendous debate about the health of our ecosystems and nothing is more central in the see-saw of environmental discussion than our forests. Practically everyone has identified values for our "natural" components of life, and an unprecedented array of people are playing the role of forester or ecologist.

The underlying theme of all this is "sustainability"—a serious concern about what the future will be like; how much forest we will have; and how healthy it will be. Predicting the future is often just a projection of the past and a matter of calculating what has been in decline. More than any other species, white pine has been singled out as the species that has suffered the greatest decline both in terms of absolute numbers and also in terms of its range. Some research contends that there is less than two percent as many large white pine today as there were prior to 1850. By any measure, there has been a drastic decline. The future of the white pine is in serious question.

There are several schools of thought about how to deal with the question of this tree's future. Some say the only answer is to preserve the older trees that are out there now, as though they will somehow live forever. This misguided thinking seems to assume that these trees will, in some way, cause the white pine to come back, purportedly through self-regeneration. It is a romantic theory and one that hasn't worked for the last 100 years. There is sparse evidence to suggest that this theory will work any better today or in the future. The other school of thought is that the future of white pine is chiefly dependent on regeneration. There is compelling evidence that white pine can be regenerated. The question remaining among experts is whether regeneration should be accomplished via natural seeding or through planting. (See "White Pine Regeneration Strategies Work Group Report" - Dec. 1997)

But we should back up a bit. The long void of any serious attempt to reproduce any significant amount of white pine is a black mark for forestry and silviculture in Minnesota. Even in the highest ranks of public forestry, professionals and policy makers were so disillusioned that our Minnesota Department of Natural Resources attempted in the 1980s to have reference to white pine removed from sections of public law. For some of us it was hard to understand whether professionals were so embarrassed by their neglect of white pine or if they were truly convinced that it was just too hopeless. Another explanation might be that forestry had long ridden a crest of enthusiasm for red pine. Not entirely coincidentally, a great interest in growing and reproducing aspen for the paper and newly-born wafer board industries had arisen.

However, a few of us die-hards were still determined that an initiative for white pine was necessary. In 1990, a symposium on white pine was held in Duluth. Experts and other citizens interested in white pine were invited to share their views on the status and future of this nearly forgotten species. Over 500 people showed up for the conference—a testimony to the great interest in white pine. It was the beginning of a change in the direction of the tide.

At this same time in recent history, an out-of-court settlement between the State of Minnesota and environmental litigators over the locating of a new wood-consuming plant in central Minnesota caused the Department of Natural Resources to develop guidelines for old-growth and extended rotation forests. White pine has been the centerpiece of these guidelines; thousands of acres have been set aside as "old growth" forest or are being held for study. During these years the sale of white pine stumpage from state forest lands had almost ceased and by 1995, was only a fraction of what it was 10 years earlier. (See Table 1 on page 33)

Unfortunately, the preservationist approach to guaranteeing white pine in the future Minnesota forest has done very little to increase this species' presence.

TABLE 1
DNR TIMBER PROGRAM
PINE SAW TIMBER SOLD (MBF)

Year	Pine Species	Red Pine	White Pine	Total
1989	4,001.4	1,008.4	333.2	5,343.0
1990	3,761.6	642.1	270.3	4,674.0
1991	3,102.0	738.1	236.3	4,076.4
1992	1,728.0	986.8	124.7	2,839.5
1993	1,876.8	729.8	92.2	2,698.8
1994	2,465.0	639.6	106.8	3,211.4
1995	1,707.0	626.7	43.8	2,377.5

Preservation has not been the answer. Trying to save old trees has not resulted in any significant restoration of white pine. If it had, the last five or six decades would certainly have shown us a great deal more reproduction.

White pine is a disturbance-related species. All evidence suggests that in the dynamics of forest succession, it is at times of disturbance (fire, windstorm, or harvest) that white pine reproduces. In the absence of natural disturbance, white pine is dependent on silviculture (man's help in producing and tending). This is what **"Bringing Back the White Pine"** is really about.

SECTION

4

CHAPTER 3

WHITE PINE SILVICULTURE

⇶Discouraging Factors

Although Minnesotans have never lost their love of
white pine, several factors have served to discourage
landowners and managers from bringing back this
favorite tree species.

First, a common ethic existed well into this century to
continue to clear the land and push back the wilderness.
A conservation ethic developed at the turn of the 20th
century as evidenced by the creation of a national forest. (The Chippewa National Forest was created in 1902
and is the oldest east of the Rockies.) The Minnesota
Legislature created a forest commission in 1895 to
enforce laws to control forest fires. But these early
efforts did not focus on the task of quickly and completely regenerating the endless acreages that had been
cutover. This is even more obvious, considering that significant amounts of land where white pine best grew
were also fair agricultural and pasture lands—
Minnesota's settlers were dogged about farming.

The second factor serving to discourage white pine
regeneration was the introduction of blister rust disease
in 1916. Early efforts to eradicate this disease were
deemed unsuccessful because the host for the disease,

the gooseberry plant (Ribes Spp.), was too pervasive and the cost of controlling it too high.

A third discouraging factor to bringing back the white pine has been the explosion of the white-tail deer population which feed on young white pine. The disturbance of the forest following logging activities in Minnesota during the past 100 years has provided wonderful habitat for deer. They have thrived well around the intermingled farms and forest openings that checkerboard much of the white pine's traditional range. Until recently, little has been said about the damage of browsing to white pine because the browsing had little effect on larger-sized white pine trees. Today, browsing is a well-known problem and a deterrent in bringing back white pine because the focus for restoration is regeneration through the establishment and care of seedlings. It is the browsing of the terminal bud of seedlings that is so devastating.

The final factor discouraging landowners and managers from making the commitment to white pine restoration is the seemingly impossible task of controlling brush and other ground cover plants. This was "naturally" done in an earlier age by periodic fires. Lack of fire has caused forest types to convert, in general, to deciduous plants; the composition of Minnesota forestlands has changed more and more to an aspen/northern hardwood type. Aspen is easy to regenerate; white pine is difficult. Under these circumstances, successional pathways of Minnesota's forests tend toward domination by hardwood species.

The enlarging public discussion on restoring white pine speaks to the fact that people truly love the tree, but a serious paradox has developed. This penchant for white pine has placed tremendous attention on preservation, in hopes that the remnants will regenerate a new white pine forest. This is unlikely to succeed and the theory obscures the critical fact that white pine restoration is really a matter of regeneration, requiring tremendous commitment and investment.

The future for white pine—of any abundance in Minnesota—has to do with methodically and religiously carrying out well-thought plans and rigorous silviculture. It requires up-front commitment, disciplined execution, and a willingness to stick with it.

Restoring significant amounts of white pine to the Minnesota landscape must be more than a debate about healthy ecosystems and natural environments. It must be an ethic expressed in a commitment. It is not for the faint-hearted. But it can be done.

Silvicultural Considerations

In his 1986 edition of the textbook, "The Practice of Silviculture," David M. Smith defines this professional forestry concept as the "art of producing and tending a forest." Certainly, the growing of white pine fits this definition. Growing white pine is all about producing (regenerating) the species; tending to it takes forestry to its culminating level. A lot has been written about white pine silviculture and yet both professional land managers and landowners seem to lack all of the knowledge they would like to have as they get serious about getting out there and doing it.

In its December 1996 report to the Commissioner of the Minnesota DNR, the White Pine Strategies Work Group alluded to this fact. The report said: *"Much is known about regenerating and managing white pine, but not all of it is readily available to land owners and resource managers."* The report went on to say: *"State-of-the-art recommendations on white pine regeneration and management should be available to all landowners. The range of ease/difficulty with the regeneration and management of white pine from one type of site to another should be addressed, and information should be provided on appropriate prescriptions for each type of site."*

In saying that "much is known" about white pine silviculture, the report was acknowledging that published information exists, such as "A Silvicultural Guide for White Pine in the Northeast," by Lancaster and Leak. Other publications are available in forestry libraries. Likely, the greatest wealth of information is stored in various unpublished guidelines and management prescriptions that have been written by foresters of state departments of natural resources and the U.S. Forest Service. Another important source of information and experience in white pine management in more recent years is the work of the Menominee Tribal Enterprises of Wisconsin. Their very successful efforts to grow white pine seem to be based on prescriptions designed by Lancaster and Leak, but are also tied closely with Wisconsin's "Habitat Type" site classification system. It should also be noted that the Minnesota DNR has a program called, "Cover Type Guidelines for White Pine."

In what was probably the most exhaustive analysis of silvicultural systems for regenerating and managing white pine in Minnesota, a sub-group of the White Pine Strategies Work Group that had research experience and extensive field expertise, outlined the more critical silvicultural considerations for the entire work group. Among the numerous recommendations put forth by these experts was the importance of matching the level of intensity which landowners/managers would be willing to put into white pine programs with the desired degree of success.

Much of the advice given by this group was based on the landowners'/managers' knowledge of what regeneration and management prescriptions to use to get the desired results. The group concluded: *"There is no 'one' best solution to increasing white pine in Minnesota. Instead, there are multiple options for accomplishing this, driven by the sites ecological potential, stage of successional development, and the landowners goals. . . . Identifying ecological potential (of sites) should improve managers' success ratio..."*

Site factors—location, aspect, soils, and a full range of biophysical and ecological features—are at the core of white pine silviculture. In a few words, landowner Rachel Jordan said it well for all silviculture, while acknowledging her accomplishments as National Tree Farmer of the Year for 1997 at the Wisconsin Woodland Owners Association annual meeting: *"Site is the dictator of success."*

The diagram (Figure 1) on pages 42 and 43 further details some of the reasons (perspectives) why landowners and managers choose to regenerate white pine, and it explains some attendant silvicultural considerations that will likely need to be addressed to accomplish the desired goals.

The White Pine Regeneration Strategies Work Group, in its report, "Minnesota's White Pine," highlighted three well-established silvicultural systems for regenerating white pine. (See Appendix). Two of the methods, *shelterwood* and *seed tree*, typically rely on natural seeding. However, seedling establishment might be preceded by reproduction cutting and/or site preparation.

The third suggested method of regeneration highlighted by the Work Group is *planting*. Although planting is normally associated with sites where a species is not populous (parents or regeneration), it can also be employed in a *shelterwood* scenario. In this case, the purpose of the shelter is not for seeding, but to supply the appropriate cover for the desired growing environment. This is often referred to as the *irregular shelterwood* method. The Rajala system explained in the following chapters is such a system.

There are important differences between silvicultural systems and the reasons for choosing one over another. Just as important are the methods of establishing and caring for regeneration and they will differ. These "elements" and "steps" are discussed in detail in Chapters 4 and 5.

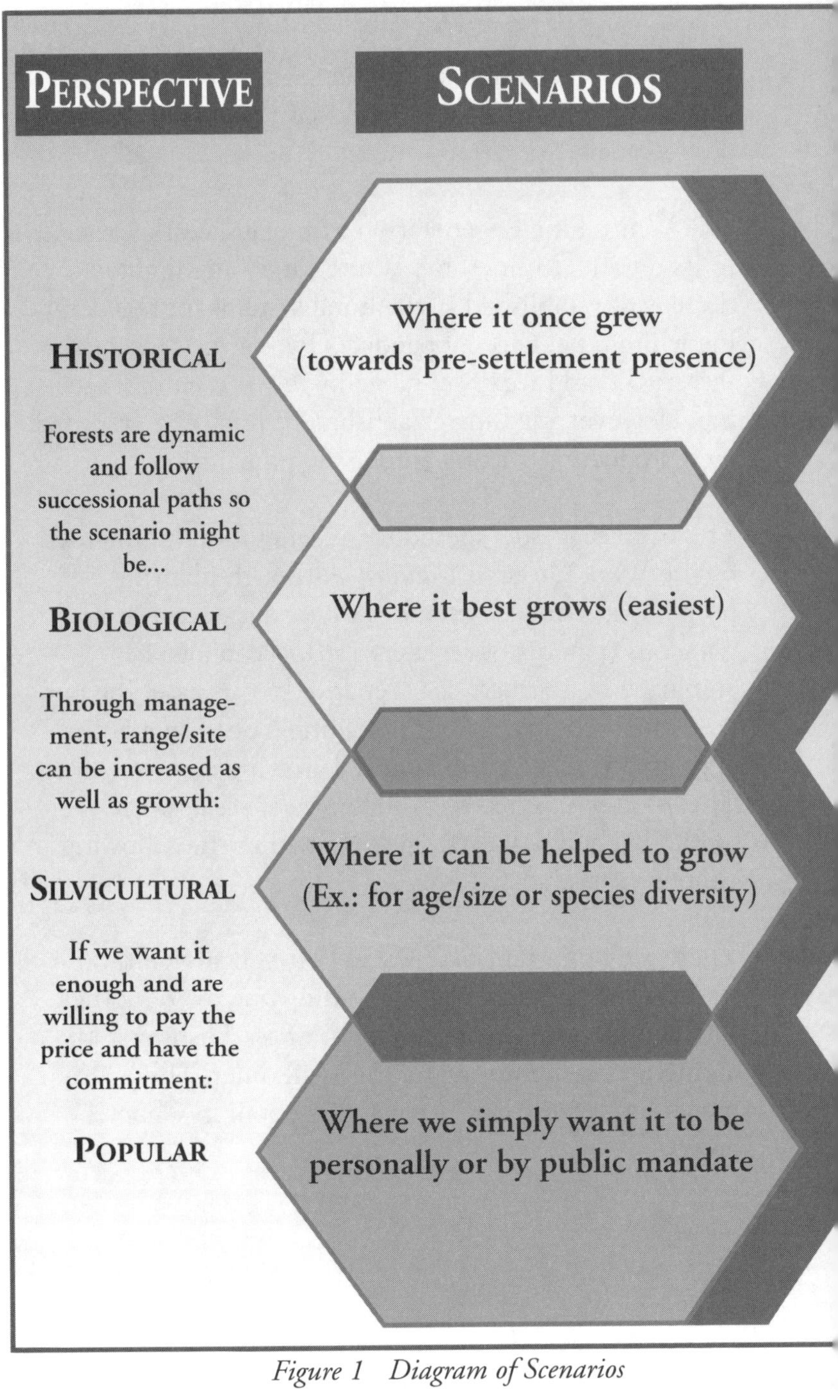

PERSPECTIVE	SCENARIOS
HISTORICAL	Where it once grew (towards pre-settlement presence)
Forests are dynamic and follow successional paths so the scenario might be...	
BIOLOGICAL	Where it best grows (easiest)
Through management, range/site can be increased as well as growth:	
SILVICULTURAL	Where it can be helped to grow (Ex.: for age/size or species diversity)
If we want it enough and are willing to pay the price and have the commitment:	
POPULAR	Where we simply want it to be personally or by public mandate

Figure 1 Diagram of Scenarios

CONSIDERATIONS

DO WE KNOW WHERE IT GREW AND ITS ABUNDANCE? ARE LAND USE/MANAGEMENT CHANGES IRREVERSIBLE?

WHAT IS A SITE'S ECOLOGICAL POTENTIAL? AT WHAT STAGE IN SUCCESSIONAL DEVELOPMENT IS THE EXISTING STAND/SITE?

IN MANAGEMENT, WHAT ARE THE DESIRED FUTURE CONDITIONS? WHAT ROLE WILL WHITE PINE PLAY? WHAT TOOLS ARE AVAILABLE?

WHY AND HOW BADLY DO WE WANT WHITE PINE ON A SITE/IN A LANDSCAPE? ARE WE WILLING TO COMMIT THE MONEY AND EFFORT TO BE SUCCESSFUL? HOW WILL SUCCESS BE MEASURED?

CHAPTER 4

REGENERATION SYSTEMS

⇗Natural Seeding Methods

Certainly the least costly way of regenerating white pine is through natural seeding. It is also the least certain in terms of results.

Elements for natural seeding

Let's look at seven critical elements of natural seeding regeneration (See Table 2):

Site/soils - The proper combination of moisture and nutrient levels will affect survival and growth. (See Figure 2)

Seed trees - There must be sufficient seed trees of a quality to produce cones and seed.

Seed quality - There will be cone crops every four to six years on average that will provide viable seed.

Seed bed - The ground must be in a condition to germinate the seed (i.e. scarified or disturbed). Soil quality and moisture regimes are other factors.

Sunlight - There must be sufficient sunlight.

Competition - There must be some agent for releasing competitive ground vegetation.

Seedling care - Finally, something must be done to keep deer from browsing the buds of the seedlings.

TABLE 2
ELEMENTS OF REGENERATION SYSTEMS

Natural seeding method	Planting method
Site/soils	Site/Soils
Seed Trees (Parents)	Seedlings (Planting stock)
Seed quality	Site preparation
Seed bed	Planting techniques
Sunlight	Sunlight
Competition	Competition
Seedling care	Protection
	Pathological pruning
	Tree spacing/Thinning
	Costs/Economics

Steps to regeneration through natural seeding

There is extensive literature available about natural seeding regeneration. (See "References" and "Work Group Report" in the **Appendix**.) The following are the steps that we have found to be the most essential here in Minnesota:

1. Select advantageous sites and soils (See Figure 2 for site prescription index. See Chapter 5 "Planting").

2. Select seed tree opportunities where several or more healthy, generally blister rust- free parents are available. Parents more than 50 years-old and less than 150 years-old are preferable because they have exhibited some natural resistance to blister rust and, up to 150 years, are strong cone and seed producers. It is important that several parent trees

WHITE PINE SITE PRESCRIPTIONS

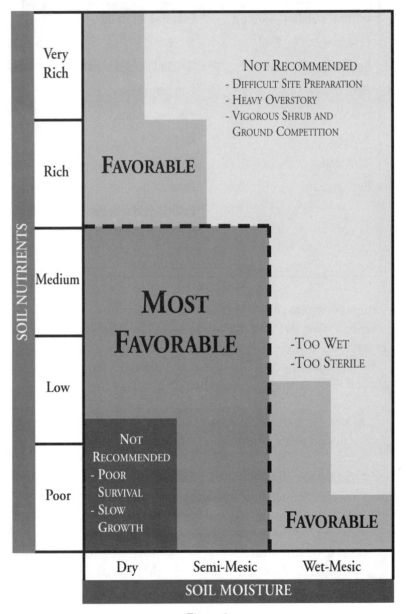

Figure 2

are available, otherwise the trees will self-pollinate and the seedlings may suffer from mutations.

Trees have genes. The characteristics of these genes show in the qualities of form, rate of growth, and overall healthiness. Seed quality will directly mimic these qualities. However, pathogens can also affect seed viability. Rule of thumb: Good seed comes from good parent trees.

3. Prior to a predicted cone-producing year (white pine cones take two years to mature; they are green the first year), prepare the site by scarifying the ground under the parents.

    Scarifying can be accomplished by dragging, disking, or prescribed burning. Selective harvesting around the parents is a very successful method of site preparation because, in addition to providing scarification of the soil if done when the ground is not frozen or snow covered, the harvesting thins the overstory (canopy) to allow greater amounts of sunlight to reach the ground. Additionally, harvesting, scarification, or herbicide application sets back competitive ground vegetation that would otherwise compete with the seedlings for sunlight, nutrients, and moisture. Remember, parents will typically cast seed 200 feet laterally (often 500 feet down prevailing winds) so be liberal about enlarging the scarified area.

4. After successful germination of seedlings, reduce the canopy to a maximum of 50 percent crown closure. The early years of seedling growth are critical; sufficient sunlight is necessary. Although white pine is considered moderately shade tolerant, this is only a generalization and is more true for survival and competing in established

stands. For the seedlings' early years, it is absolutely necessary to provide a minimum of 50 percent sunlight. Caution: Inversely, the canopy is important to the young seedlings and saplings to prevent soils from becoming too dry and to catch summer dew—like an umbrella. Heavy dew causes the young tree's microclimate to be susceptible to blister rust and white pine tip weevil infestations. So, the balance of some shade, but not too much, is a fine one and should be carefully addressed.

5. As the seedlings grow, it is critical to their survival to control competitive ground-level vegetation. Control is best accomplished by manually removing (killing or retarding) the woody plants, such as hazel and maple sprouts that naturally invade these sites. Ironically, the very best white pine sites are often the best brush and hardwood shrub/sapling sites.

6. Browsing by herbivores is a serious problem for seedlings and saplings. With the use of bud caps, prevent the browsing by deer (and to some degree, rabbits) of the terminal bud of the seedling. This terminal bud is the most critical bud. Although tree tubes, shelters, and protective mesh may be used, bud caps are far less expensive, effective, and more friendly to the plant.

Bud caps are pieces of regular, gloss-grade paper, approximately 2-1/2 x 4-1/2 inches in size. The caps are fastened horizontally around the terminal bud, rather loosely, with the use of a standard staple gun and two or three staples (See Illustration on p. 78). Care should be taken to include only one (the terminal) bud or leader in the bud cap. However, catch several needles in the staple placement to help guarantee that the bud cap will not be easily detached.

Bud caps should be applied during September and October each fall after the leader is fully grown for the season and the new bud has hardened. This is a time prior to the first snowfall when deer turn to the buds to browse. If applied correctly, the bud cap will still be there to protect the seedlings during spring thaw—a time at which the deer seem to relish the white pine terminal bud even more. The little trees need to be bud capped anew each year in the fall until the saplings are approximately five feet tall and out of range of the deer's reach.

With either method of regeneration, (natural seeding or planting), follow-up care of the seedlings is crucial. For as prolific as white pine seeds take root, they have many natural enemies to fight. Without help from the landowner or land manager, the young trees will have difficulty growing and thriving. Growth is slow during the first five years—often only several inches annually in years one and two. Then they will grow six to 12 inches annually for several years. As the roots take hold and the needle mass develops, the seedlings become very vigorous and growth jumps to 12 to 24 inches annually. It is not uncommon to see leaders up to 30 inches and more as the seedlings turn to saplings.

It is during the early years of slow growth that most seedlings die; thus, this is a critical stage. Protecting against deer browse and providing sunlight by releasing the seedlings from ground competition (mostly brush and shrubs) will make the difference. In natural seeding situations, where most of the process just happens, it is easy to ignore how critical these factors are. This likely explains why natural regeneration has been so unsuccessful in Minnesota over the last century. Walk away forestry has not worked.

Finally, the cultural practices of pruning and thinning are also important to ensure long term survival and growth. Details on these practices are included in the chapter "Planting."

Planting Method

Every year, approximately 1.4 million white pine seedlings are currently planted throughout Minnesota. This modest number is a far cry from what landowners and land managers could be planting; at this rate, only about 1,500 to 2,000 acres of land will be restored to white pine annually. Planting and after-care are expensive, consequently many land managers have ignored white pine and chosen to raise other "low maintenance" species such as red pine.

Red pine planting is also expensive but the practice has become so common that Minnesota has major amounts of red pine plantations. There are 202,000 acres listed in the 1990 Forest Inventory Assessment data. ("An Analysis of Minnesota's Fifth Forest Resources Inventory, 1990." p. 12) There are probably less than 5,000 acres of white pine plantation. Red pine plantations are monocultures and generally include only one age class per stand. Although this system is heralded for fast growth and better economic value, today's demand for more diverse forest habitats is challenging the practice of plantation forestry.

White pine is more complicated and expensive to regenerate and differs from red pine in the "where" and the "how" of planting. White pine can grow in partial shade. This single fact creates opportunities for white pine that red pine doesn't have.

In fact, some of the most successful white pine planting is where it is underplanted below a canopy of larger trees—most often trees of some other species. White pine really can be the consummate species when trying to find something to get growing underneath, or to introduce a new age class while maintaining and aging stands of hardwoods or pine through the practices of thinning, group selection, or single tree selection.

Theory aside, white pine is simply a good choice when it is desirable to add a new species or a new age class. This would often be impossible through natural seeding regeneration for lack of parent seed trees. However, planting white pine seedlings in the understory can be the perfect answer.

It is not likely that the debate among foresters and ecologists about which method of regeneration—natural seeding or planting—will quickly be resolved. It has been going on for a long time and there is no, "one right answer."

Table 2 shows the critical elements for each method. There are similarities; yet, major differences do exist. These differences should be considered on a site-by-site basis and should not control or affect anyone's overall commitment to regenerate white pine.

Unfortunately, these differences have affected policy for many years. Reams of research data have been collected and significant scientific and professional discussion has been carried out. The overall result has been one of: "We don't have all the answers yet." Any major public policy initiative or incentive for restoration through regeneration has been thwarted.

Unfortunate? Yes! There is sufficient good information on how to grow white pine. If we want to do it, there is no compelling reason not to. It is really a matter of "getting out there and doing it."

The pieces of the puzzle will fall into place readily. Natural seeding regeneration is the least difficult (yet also least successful), whereas planting requires more steps; consequently, more information is needed. In addition to the steps and methodology suggested here, a bibliographical reference of extensive regeneration and silvicultural information can be found in the Appendix.

Elements for planting white pine

As mentioned earlier, there are more elements to regenerating white pine through planting than through natural seeding. (See Table 2.) They include the following:

Site/soils - Selection of the most advantageous sites and soils is important, not only for seedling response and growth, but also for their great bearing on competition to new seedlings and, ultimately, the seedlings' survival.

Planting stock - Seedlings, both bare-root stock and containerized seedlings, are the most common planting stock. Direct seeding can be a choice under some conditions. Availability of planting stock is a factor, but source and quality are also critical to survival, health, and growth. Seedlings can be purchased from the Minnesota Department of Natural Resources and from private nurseries. However, because of increased interest in planting white pine, shortages in stock do occur. Arrangements should be made for acquiring seedlings—through public or private sources—many months in advance of planting time.

Site preparation - Getting the site ready for planting is both a matter of sound forest stand management (underplanting method) and an important factor for seedling response, early survival, and growth in the critical first years. A number of site preparation options are available in the planting method.

Planting technique - Method of planting is probably the most variable and subjective element in regenerating white pine through planting. But no matter which method is used, (i.e. hand, machine, early or late and optional spacing choices) proper care of stock and careful attention to essential details are critical to success.

Sunlight - Adequate sunlight is important to seedling growth. Although white pine is rated as moderately shade tolerant, seedling vigor is dependent on sunlight. Rapid growth of seedlings is extremely important to biological success and also has an equally important economic impact. (See "4" under Natural Seeding Method.)

Competition - When properly planted on correct sites and soils, seedlings take root well and early survival is high. But competitive vegetation will also do well, especially the brush and maple saplings that are very accustomed to growing in the understory. To have any measure of success, this competition must be dealt with.

Protection - There are four major natural enemies of white pine. All four are most threatening in the early years of the white pine's life. Competition from other vegetation is mentioned in the previous paragraph. Deer browse is another serious enemy of white pine seedlings and has been the least understood and acknowledged. Wherever there are deer, seedlings and young saplings must be protected.

Blister rust is a serious enemy of white pine too. But it has been grossly over-reacted to by most foresters. It is important to know that there is no absolutely rust-resistant white pine stock. There are only degrees of genetic resistance to blister rust. The ultimate success, at least during the first 30 years of life, can be greatly improved by underplanting and growing white pine under a partial canopy of other trees.

The fourth enemy of white pine is the white pine tip weevil. Underplanting and growing white pine below a canopy greatly reduces the presence of the tip weevil infestation.

Pathological pruning - Pruning to remove lower limbs has a number of important benefits in growing white pine. First, it helps keep a drier, more airy microclimate at the base of the young tree. Also, pruning lower limbs greatly improves trunk quality by eliminating knots. Smooth, clean trunks also provide better bark protection from other diseases and insects.

Tree spacing and thinning - A range of professional opinion exists about how many seedlings should be planted per acre, and how often and how much white pine stands should be thinned. Both biological and economic factors are involved and both should be thoroughly considered before setting up the planting pattern and before thinning.

Cost/Economics - All the elements mentioned, including "spacing" and "thinning," have a great bearing on costs and, ultimately, the economics of white pine regeneration. These must be understood by the landowner/land manager before committing to planting white pine.

SECTION
5

PLANTING METHOD GUIDELINES

SELECTING SITES
Various Cover Type Opportunities

Example

STEPS TO PLANTING
Site Preparation

Selection of planting stock

Planting techniques

STEPS TO PROTECTION AND CARE
Providing sunlight

Release from competition

Protection

Pruning

Thinning and spacing

OTHER COVER TYPES

COSTS/ECONOMICS

CHAPTER 5

PLANTING METHOD GUIDELINES

The practice of forestry is not exacting because there are so many variables with which to deal. Through study, research, and experience, some techniques have proven to be the most successful, and help guide the growing and tending of forests. Regenerating white pine in Minnesota depends on doing a combination of things right. Hence, a set of guidelines to "guide" the process is helpful. The following steps are methodologies that we have found to be most important; they are based on many years of trial and error. They are not absolute or conclusive, but they should serve as valuable guidelines to help improve the degree of success in planting and raising white pine.

Step: Selecting Sites

It was mentioned earlier that planting white pine is more difficult and more costly than natural seeding. Even so, planting has one great advantage over natural seeding. Whereas natural seeding takes place randomly in the locations where seed trees may be present, planting can and should take place specifically where site and soils are most favorable for the establishment and grow- ing of white pine.

Underplanting is one of the most advantageous techniques of regenerating white pine. It also provides the opportunity to keep managing the cover type or species that is already established on the site, and most likely improving growth and health through a thinning or sanitation treatment. When white pine is then introduced in the understory, we have the best of both worlds—maintaining and improving the present forest cover type while simultaneously getting a valuable new stand started underneath.

Silvicultural methods range from thinning to shelterwood opportunities. An explanation of different methods is included in the Appendix. However, picking appropriate underplanting sites can be challenging and confusing.

Figure 2 shows how moving across a scale of soil nutrient values versus a companion scale of moisture regimes helps determine the best range of regeneration opportunities. To be successful, this information should be carefully considered. Having the right combination of site and soils, as measured by soil nutrient levels and moisture regimes, can largely guarantee regeneration success.

Various cover type opportunities
Selecting the "right" site (and soils) is the first, and likely most important step for underplanting. Consider the following cover type opportunities:

1. **Under an overstory of northern hardwoods, oak or birch,** where enough thinning can be done to allow sufficient sunlight for white pine to grow. Often we

want to be able to maintain these cover types, but the stands need sanitation and thinning for the purpose of putting additional growth on the crop (higher quality) trees. Extending out the life of the primary stands to gain additional growth normally means delaying regeneration. This is frustrating because the long time between rotations gets even longer. Managers repeatedly wonder how to overlap stands (or rotations) to decrease the long time frames. Because white pine is relatively shade tolerant, it can be an excellent choice for a high value stand to establish underneath hardwoods. Proper thinning is critical and attention must be given to soil nutrient values and soil moisture conditions (See Figure 2) in choosing the best opportunities and setting up the necessary prescriptions for success.

2. **In overmature (and perhaps "off-site") aspen types.** As a starting point, these sites can offer an opportunity to salvage something from the stand, even though many of the aspen trees might simply be left to natural mortality. The gaps created by removal of trees provide opportunities (holes) to underplant white pine. The remaining trees provide the necessary canopy and, as they diminish, a natural process of release takes place over a period of time to help the white pine grow. Once the suckering from the harvested aspen trees has been treated, there shouldn't be much competition from young aspen since aspen are not good direct seeders. Also, aspen crowns don't seem to respond to thinning. Therefore, the upper canopies will continue to open rather than close back as other hardwood canopies do.

3. **Interplant in established balsam fir types.** We often find sites where the balsam fir is predominant and yet have plenty of holes in the stand, or where there are two or three age classes. Because balsam fir have spired crowns, adequate amounts of sunlight can reach the ground to help the new seedlings, yet there is still enough lower tree crown to help prevent heavy summer dew. We often see excellent natural conifer regeneration in these sites; many times these are old pasture lands or field edges that want to return to forest cover over a period of time and consequently have a mixture of age classes. These sites might also have some grass competition, but white pine seedlings can compete through grass if there is sufficient sunlight. Note: If wild raspberry invades these sites it will choke the white pine seedlings; it must be dealt with.

4. **Under overstories of larger white or red pine that have fully develope**d crowns but still have enough gaps to allow for planting seedlings and for sunlight to reach the ground. As these older, established stands mature, they thin themselves out via disease or natural selection. Prescribed thinning through harvesting can also produce the same effect of opening up the stands and reducing the crown coverage. The very presence of the older pine indicates a preferable pine site and the new seedlings should do well. Certainly, these sites should also be considered good natural regeneration opportunities.
   Surprisingly, however, they don't typically "just happen"—especially on the more mesic (wet) sites. What happens more often, as these stands thin out, hazel brush rapidly fills in and quickly chokes out

the pine regeneration. These preferred sites also often have a thick layer of needle duff that prevents natural seedlings from getting their roots set in the mineral soil below. Properly thinning the overstory, controlling the brush, and planting seedlings with their roots deeply into mineral soil overcomes these problems and makes these sites excellent opportunities for regeneration. Putting white pine in underneath doesn't add much to the species diversity, but it certainly adds to the structural diversity by adding another age class.

5. **Underplanting or interplanting in areas where there has been catastrophic occurrence.** Although sites of wildfires are uncommon today, they provide excellent planting sites—especially if there is some remaining overstory. A major benefit of fire is that it sets back competitive ground vegetation. Windthrow openings and sites that are opened when canopy trees die from insects, disease, or natural selection also provide opportunities for introducing white pine through planting.

6. **Planting gaps and openings along streams, rivers, and lakes.** Beaver periodically harvest aspen, birch, willow, and ash that typically grow in these mesic areas. The openings that beaver create are opportunities for planting white pine, since the beaver rarely chew on conifers. These critical riparian sites need to have long-lived trees mixed in to help stabilize banks with their massive root structures. The tall and full canopies of white pine also provide excellent shade to keep the adjacent water and microclimate cool.

White pine grow over an extremely broad range of sites and soils. They can place their roots down into a minor crack in a rock ledge, grow on sugar sand, or flourish in the mossy carpet of a black spruce swamp. This is one of the amazing qualities of the species. For landowners and land managers, the options we have in planting white pine are many if we are willing to settle for a range of degrees of difficulty and success. Certainly, the results will vary from highly successful initial survival to very low survival and poor growth, depending on the site we choose.

The key point in planting white pine is to know what each site opportunity could result in and then to decide if the effort and investment are worth it in terms of the predictable results. Each site will have its advantages and disadvantages. These can be recognized first by general landscape and site characteristics that are highlighted in the preceding examples. Equally important is to consider the growing capacity of sites and soils as exhibited in Figure 2. But also very important are the preparatory planting and follow up methods that were mentioned as "elements" in white pine planting techniques on pages 54 through 56.

When all these factors are considered together and we have made our decision (our commitment), then it is time to "go do it." So many professional foresters and landowners have gotten close but have held back because they felt they needed just one more answer; or else they had one last reservation that served to discourage them from doing it.

What a shame! Planting and establishing white pine is difficult and highly technical. But white pine really wants to grow in so many places right here in Minnesota. Sure, we will make some mistakes and have a few setbacks. But with desire and commitment, the results can be surprisingly good and the sense of satisfaction tremendous.

So, let's "go do it." The following is one example that takes us through the planting, step by step.

Example: Planting under an advanced age pine overstory

Planting white pine under an overstory of advanced age red and/or white pine is one of the most favorable opportunities for regeneration. Normally the soils and moisture regimes are right where there is pine already on the site. Therefore, the first step, picking the right site, is already well-determined. (Note: Hardwood sites are much more difficult and are discussed later.)

Steps to Planting

Site preparation

Getting the site ready to plant has two important aspects. First, it requires creating enough gap in the overstory to provide the necessary sunshine. There is still a lot of debate about how much overstory can be left before it is "too much." The Menominee of Wisconsin have done a lot of experimentation and believe that the overstory should be reduced to 20 percent cover so that the seedlings are relatively "free to grow" Here in Minnesota, we prefer maintaining approximately 50 percent crown cover. This sacrifices

JIM KASPER ©

some early growth potential, but helps protect the seedlings from blister rust and tip weevil, and greatly reduces the amount of Rubus species (raspberry and blackberry) with which seedlings would have to compete.

The second part of this step, disturbing the site, involves reducing the competition from brush and getting ground scarification. To accomplish this without undue cost, we look for opportunities where harvesting something on the site, if even lightly, can accomplish this. Removing only three to four cords per acre gets the brush knocked down and the soil scratched around if the harvester is conscious of the purpose.

Obviously, the combination of bare ground and summer-time harvesting best accomplishes the purpose. But good, common sense is also necessary—overstory trees must not be scarred and the site should not be unduly rutted from the harvesting operation. Most sites where pine is currently present consist of soils that are lighter, drier, and well-drained. They are ideal for summer harvesting and rutting should not be a problem. Just the same, the early summer season is a time when the sap is running vigorously and the bark is very tender. Great care must be taken not to injure the existing trees when operating among them.

Traditional pine sites, because they are normally drier, may not have as much ground plant cover as more mesic sites. Consequently, even with a minimum of scarification, the ground should be ready for planting. It will also be prime for natural seeding if a cone crop is present in a year or two. This is the one site where we would be willing to use containerized or smaller seedlings such as 2-0 (two years old). But we would still be conscious of potential invasion of hazel brush and raspberries. We would delay planting one year and use herbicides the first year after site preparation, then plant the second year.

Selection of planting stock
Both containerized and bare root nursery stock are available. If bare root is the choice, it should be at least 3-0 or 2-2 (two years in the seed bed and then an additional two years in a transplant bed). Experience shows that undersized seedlings suffer from too much ground cover competition and cannot find enough sunlight in the critical first years after planting.

There is currently a shortage of white pine seedlings grown in Minnesota nurseries. On many sites we prefer bare root nursery stock that is at least three years-old and transplants, if possible. This preference is because the seedling will then be both taller and have finer roots (transplants). Experience tells us that we will generally get these seedlings up through ground competition and out of deer browse range sooner.

Containerized stock (plugs) is also available in white pine and works well and is easier to plant than bare root. Plugs are also lower in cost than advanced bare root stock. However, the trade off is the additional growing time it generally takes to get them through the hazards mentioned above.

There is significant debate about the importance of climatized stock—in other words, stock obtained from

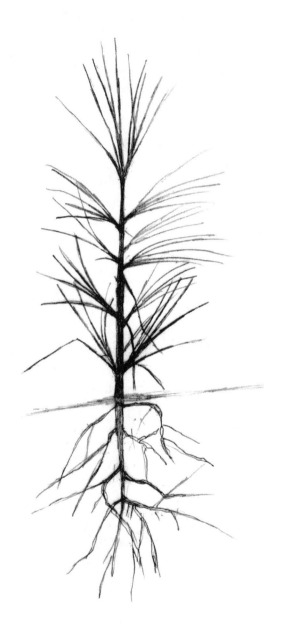

white pine parentage of local, or similar climate. In times of shortages, we have purchased stock from nurseries in Wisconsin and Michigan and have experienced no problems with survival or growth. The common thought among silviculturists is that non-resident stock can be safely planted most places in the general range, if latitude is about the same. Apparently, similar climate is the key factor.

Planting techniques
Almost without exception, white pine is hand-planted with a planting bar. The bar needs to have a spade width of at least three inches to make a large enough hole for all the roots of the seedling. By totally embedding a 3-inch by 6-inch long bar into the soil, the hole will be large enough to nicely engulf all the roots if the bar is wiggled back and forth a little. When the seedling is placed in the hole, the roots should be oriented straight down and buried deeply enough to cover the root collar. Exposed roots and shallow planting cause desiccation; survival and early growth will be affected.

Seedlings must be carried well-covered in a moist planting bag or pail and should not be exposed to open air or sunlight for more than a few seconds. Do not carry seedlings around in the hand. Make the hole and then reach into the bag for the seedling and immediately get it into the ground.

Next, seal the hole by making an adjacent tamping hole or apply a very heavy heel stomp to totally seal the hole. No air should be allowed to get to the roots. Careful planting will result in fewer seedlings planted in a day, but much higher survival rates. It is far more efficient to

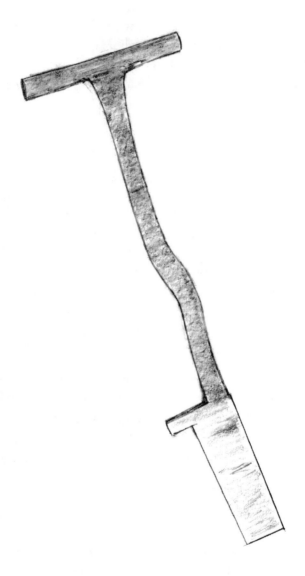

plant 1,000 seedlings per day and have 900 survive than to plant 2,000 per day and have only 6- to 7,000 survive.

The question of planting spacing is often asked. Normally when planting under an overstory the goal will be at least 800 seedlings planted per acre. This represents a distance between seedlings of approximately six to eight feet (up to 25 percent of the area is unplanted because of slash and overstory trees). Under average survival rates, 800 seedlings per acre will allow for mortality and some thinning in future years. Experience shows that 60 percent of the cost of planting is the fixed cost per acre of site preparation and management. The other 40 percent is variable, like the cost per seedling and per tree planting cost. It is only common sense then to be sure to plant enough seedlings per acre to guarantee adequate stocking. At a minimum, plant in such a way that there will be 600 surviving seedlings 10 years hence.

Both biological and economic factors determine the number of seedlings that we plant and the number of trees that we want as the stand develops. Economically, we want the maximum number that the site and conditions will efficiently grow. Biologically, we must recognize soil, moisture, and climatic factors that control the proper spacing to maximize health and growth. The following table is an approximate schedule for an average site index of 60 and the number of stems that should be present at various stand age levels:

STOCKING LEVEL

Age 0	Seedlings planted	800-1,000 per acre
Age 10	After allowing for early mortality (desiccation, browse, competition)	600
Age 20	After allowing for additional mortality (blister rust, snow breakage)	500
Age 40	After allowing for mortality and early commercial thinning	400
Age 60	After allowing for basal area thinning	300
Age 80	" "	125
Age 100	" "	60
Age 120	" "	40

⫸ Steps to Protection and Care

Providing sunlight

Adequate sunlight is essential to successful white pine regeneration and growth. The seedlings can survive a year or two in heavy shade but the more sunlight they receive, the faster they will grow. This fact is of great importance because competitive vegetation and browsing are so detrimental to white pine growth—the faster the seedlings can reach sapling height of five to six feet, the greater the success. We have planted hundreds of thousands of seedlings under 70 percent crown cover—the old standard—only to find out that without more sunlight tree growth was extremely slow . . . 2 to 4 inches in height per year. It was literally impossible for the trees to stay ahead of the flora and brush. Even worse, deer browsing was so bad that, each year that the seedlings were small enough to browse, it resulted in further loss in stocking.

Open field planting would provide the maximum sunlight but the trade off is a greatly increased probability of blister rust and tip weevil damage.

Release from competition
Competition from other vegetation is the "other side of the coin" from sunlight in affecting how white pine seedlings and saplings grow. This competition comes from both the upper canopy and ground level plants and brush. We have already discussed the handling of the upper canopy in earlier paragraphs. Now we need to talk about the likelihood that brush, ground plants, and raspberries are going to cause significant shading that will have to be dealt with.

Although we have generally found that sites with pine on them are drier and less vegetated, we have also found that good pine sites grow abundant hazel brush. The further we move up the moisture/nutrient scale into aspen-balsam fir and finally into northern hardwood sites, the more we experience increasing amounts of maple and ironwood shrubs, plus greatly increased amounts of hardwoods. Paradoxically, the more sunlight that filters through the upper canopy, the more ground level competition there will be. This is especially true for Rubus species, particularly wild raspberry.

Four to five years after planting, this competition will likely become a problem. On the pine-type sites, some minor hand release work with a machete or pruning shears will do the trick, but where there is aspen or hardwood the shading will be much greater and will require more attention. On these latter sites we have also used a herbicide treatment, but with only limited success. While killing the competition, we also killed many white pine seedlings. If a herbicide is used, it is extremely important to work very closely with the herbicide manufacturer and applicator. As an alternative, we performed a more intensive hand release; this gave us greater success.

For this release work, we have tried brush saws, but ultimately the most successful method is criss-crossing the plantation with pruning shears and simply cutting out the undesirable competition. One person can typically release two acres a day; we have figured our costs to run approximately $30 per acre.

On the more densely vegetated sites, we have had to release a second time before the saplings reach 6 to 7 feet tall and above the height of competition. Although the cost of release is significant, keeping the seedlings "free to grow" is too important to ignore. It must be repeated: In dealing with white pine, "walk-away forestry" just doesn't work.

Experience shows that the best time to kill brush competition is during July and early August. This time of "full foliage" is the time during which the brush is most vulnerable. Unfortunately, it is also harder to find small seedlings during this time of year when they are hidden under forest vegetation. Our rule-of-thumb is to open a horizon on the sunny side that equals the distance from the tree. For example, at two feet away there should be a two-foot sunny horizon and at four feet away, a four-foot horizon, etc.

At approximately 5 to 6 feet in height, white pine will start to out-compete the brush and this part of the job is done. The exception might be on sites where there are vigorous aspen or maple saplings present. In this situation, one more release might be necessary.

Protection

Protecting seedlings from deer browsing is, indeed, a challenge! It is during the same young age of the seedlings when they're in danger of being choked for sunlight that they're equally in danger of having their terminal bud nipped off by deer as they browse for late fall and early spring food.

Although the degree of browsing will vary from year to year, deer consistently seem to crave white pine buds just at the time of the first snowfall in late autumn and when the receding snow first bares the terminal bud in the spring. We have experienced almost 100 percent

Jim Kasper ©

browsing in some sites during some years. When it goes on for several years the seedlings are so repressed that they become dwarfed by the competition and are lost. When deer are present, as they almost always are here in Minnesota, the seedlings need protection. We have tried spraying the seedlings with various types of commercial repellent and also a home-made concoction in a base of rotten eggs. Results were not good, with an average of 20 percent seedling survival.

What works is the application of a small piece of paper stapled horizontally around the terminal bud (this is the only bud that really counts). The cap is fastened with several staples that catch a few needles to hold it in place. Care should be taken to fully surround the leader and hide the bud about 1/2 inch below the upper edge of the paper (see illustration on page 78).

Also, the bud cap should be loose enough so it does not restrict the bud's vertical growth, yet tight enough to hang on. A good method is to slide the index finger over the bud and into the cap when it is being applied and stapled. This seems to allow the proper amount of clearance in the cap.

Bud caps should be applied after the seedling's buds have hardened off each fall, normally in late September. The caps will protect against fall browsing and then will still be there to protect the seedlings in the spring if they have been properly applied.

Care should be taken to include only the single terminal leader in the bud cap or else the seedlings' growth will be constricted and in some cases the seedlings will even be killed. The paper cap is typically 2-1/4" x 4-1/2" in size and from ordinary paper stock. We have tried both coated and uncoated white stock and both seem to work.

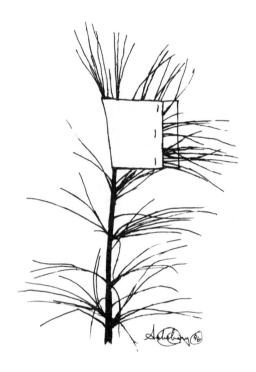

In some cases, we've experienced browsing in the first year after planting, but typically we don't apply bud caps until seedlings are at least six inches tall. We need to apply new caps each fall until the saplings are tall enough to be out of the deer's reach. We have found that to be at about 5 feet. On good sites where pine is already present, we apply bud caps for 3-5 years. Elsewhere, we have to apply them for five years and more.

Other major agents of damage to white pine seedlings are snow/ice and moisture desiccation. Snow and ice can cause significant damage to seedlings by breaking off the tops or causing severe crook to the stems. Winter moisture desiccation also can cause saplings to "brown out" badly, sometimes leading to death. Unfortunately, we don't have easy remedies for either.

Pruning

White pine seedlings and saplings grow whorls that form into branches. Normally these branches stay alive and green right down to the trunk—especially if they are growing in the open. It is through these lower branches that blister rust is most likely to attack the seedlings if it is present in the area. The spores settle on the needles of the lower limbs and then enter into the limb itself. Blister rust travels slowly (only approximately 1-1/2" per year) and if detected while only in the limbs, can be pruned off and the tree saved. (Blister rust produces a canker and causes a color change from green to red that can be readily seen). Once the canker shows on the tree trunk, there is no saving the tree.

To eliminate, or at least greatly reduce the incidence of blister rust, the lower limbs of saplings should be pruned off. This can be readily accomplished with a pair of pruning shears. Care should be taken not to prune too closely, thus tearing the thin bark of the sapling (Winter-time pruning results in less tearing of bark).

Another reason for pruning white pine is to improve the quality of the tree. This should be done periodically throughout the younger years, typically removing 2-3 whorls at a time. With a pole-saw, trees can be pruned at least to 17 feet in height which helps produce a limb-free (and thereby knot-free) log in the trunk. Typically in white pine, 1/3 of the volume is in the first 16' of the tree. If that area can be free of knots, the total value of the tree is greatly increased.

As an example, the select grade of white pine lumber sells for approximately $1,500 per MBF, whereas the average knotty grade sells for about $500 per MBF. This cultural pruning should be done during the fall or winter seasons so that the least amount of damage is done to the tender bark that exists around the limb collar. Damage seems to occur more often with the pole saw than with pruning shears; it is also much more evident on green limbs than with dry ones. Finally, a good rule of thumb for how much of the trunk to prune is a maximum of 1/2 the height, or 1/3 the live crown in any one treatment.

Thinning and spacing
To continue our example of regenerating white pine under a canopy of older pine . . . let's next address the subject of spacing and thinning. Earlier we discussed planting densities, expected survival rates, and sunlight requirements; now we should discuss the need for adequate room to grow.

Even if initial planting survival rate is high, some thinning of the young trees will naturally take place from competition, deer browse, blister rust, and ice and snow. However, under a high pine overstory, there could be enough lateral light so that between ages 30 years and 40 years the regeneration might still be so thick that thinning will be required. It is during this period that the crowns of the young trees really want to fill out and spread. We believe that there is a need to keep some gap between crowns even at this young age—maybe 3 to 4 feet—to provide for good vigor and growth.

Remember, a tree's crown width is a pretty good mirror image of its root domain. If the crowns become interlocked, it is likely that root systems are also and the trees are starting to starve each other. In a thinning at this age, there should already be some significant value in the stems being removed and in the quality of the remaining trees (keeping the stand relatively dense in prior years should have already guaranteed good tree form). Although crop tree growth has likely been temporarily compromised during this time, the effect of keeping stands relatively tight is to have produced trees with straight trunks, minimal taper, and reduced number of lower limbs.

Giving the tree crowns adequate room to grow at this stage now becomes a major priority. With this room, white pine can be one of the fastest and tallest growing trees in our Minnesota forests. We have had many opportunities to watch red and white pine grow side by side and we have repeatedly noted that white pine will outgrow red pine—both in height and girth—over a period of years.

It appears that, especially on lighter and more xeric (dry) soils, red pine will shoot up faster and put on more caliper in the first 5 to 10 years. After that, the slower-starting white pine catches up and surpasses red pine. It is also a well-established fact that white pine will ultimately grow significantly larger than red pine. We have some white pine approaching 48 inches in diameter, but we would be hard-pressed to find a red pine over 36 inches.

Because white pine trees grow large and are long-lived, they multiply in timber value many times during their extended life. Also, their large, irregular crowns have tremendous aesthetic appeal and are favorites for bald eagles and osprey. These "big tree" qualities are recognized by landowners, timbermen, tourists and forest visitors. Today, raising white pine to longer life (rotation age) and to large diameters is at the very center of the discussion of forest policy. The result being that white pine has become both the focal point and centerpiece of old growth forests. It has become one of the best and most logical species to grow into extended rotation forests(ERF).

To manage white pine to these ages and sizes, some thinning and spacing out of these large trees must take place. Whether from natural thinning or by harvesting, a smaller and smaller number of stems can survive in the course of the trees getting older and larger. Today, more than ever before, the rationale for thinning white pine stands has become greater and greater. In an earlier paragraph there is a schedule of how many white pine trees per acre are right for ideal white pine management.

Other Cover Types

We've quite thoroughly discussed planting in the pine cover type. Most of the other site types suitable for white pine planting would be handled in much the same fashion with only a few variations. However, when we move all the way up the soil nutrient and moisture scale to mesic (wet) and rich, where northern hardwoods dominate the type, the process becomes more complex.

Just the same, planting underneath a canopy of northern hardwoods is one of the best and most common opportunities that we have found for white pine. There are many good reasons to pick a northern hardwood site, including white pine's historic presence on these sites, the compatibility of soils for these two cover types, and a host of environmental and biological similarities. The best reason for this match up, we believe, is the opportunity to enhance an already desirable stand with the addition of white pine.

For example, we landowners and managers most often want to maintain our northern hardwood cover types both for their aesthetic and commercial values. Yet, these types often need silvicultural attention in the process of growing to their full potential—large, healthy trees. Suppressed and weaker trees fall out in competition, and gaps develop where non-desirable maple and hazel brush take over.

These stands, at a certain age, require more than a simple sanitation treatment. They are prime for initiating desirable regeneration underneath. We have thought long and hard about hundreds of sites and thousands of acres like this example. Our concern has always been the same: how can one get something very desirable growing down on the ground, while maintaining and improving the hardwood cover type that is already there? Planting white pine underneath can be the right answer because it can grow under partial shade.

Yes, other species, like white spruce, could be introduced. We could even encourage some of the better hard maple saplings to grow (basswood, birch, oak, or aspen would not likely do well). White pine also has the advantage of being able to fight through the upper canopy if it is still there years later. As crown gaps develop, white pine has an uncanny way of ultimately leap-frogging through the competition.

Remembering the basic elements of the white pine planting method, let's go back to the beginning and mention a few important steps.

Site and Soils
We are likely on a somewhat rolling, well-drained land-form that probably has loamy soils one to two feet deep over a coarser subsoil. By referring to Figure 2, we probably will identify the site as having soils of moderate to high nutrient value and having a moisture regime of slightly mesic. We can expect white pine to grow well here. However, hazel and maple brush will too. In fact, a whole host of ground plants will likely explode on the site once there has been some disturbance in preparation for planting the white pine. We know in advance that ground competition is something that we will need to contend with. We have picked a challenging but certainly potentially advantageous site.

Site preparation
Site preparation involves the two key elements. Assuming that this is an underplanting, the canopy has

to be a maximum of 50 percent crown cover to allow adequate sunlight. If it is higher than 50 percent, the canopy needs to be thinned, likely through a selection harvest operation. If this operation is correctly done, the canopy will be properly opened and the ground will be partially scarified if the harvest takes place when the ground is not frozen or snow-covered.

The remainder of the necessary scarification can be accomplished by using a root rake, bulldozer, or similar equipment to push away the majority of the slash. The critical element is to have some bare mineral soil exposed. Note that the slash raking also makes planting a lot easier. In some cases where straight, parallel strips are harvested, a trenching plow will provide the same result of exposing mineral soil and making room to plant.

Release from competition
Dealing with competition from shrubs and brush in northern hardwood cover types requires more attention than on other sites. We have found that, without fail, we must do a thorough job of applying herbicide on the planting site the summer before we plant.

Protection
We further find that we must rush the seedlings' growth along as fast as possible, using bud capping and overstory control, because two phenomenon are going to take place: First, the thinned hardwood canopy is going to start closing up within just a few years. Second, the maple seedlings, brush, and herbaceous growth will rapidly reinvade the planting site. More likely than not, the remedial practice of hand releasing the seedlings from ground competition and killing or removing some

intermediate canopy will be necessary. Also, it often seems that these are prime deer browse sites so thorough and consistent bud capping is critical.

Back in the days when wildfire roamed the Minnesota forest, it equalized these forces and white pine grew well and beautiful amongst the hardwood on these sites. Today, the equalizer must be our silvicultural ingenuity and persistence. This might be the very place where we landowners and managers most test our commitment to restoring white pine. Certainly it is the place where "walk-away forestry" won't work.

Costs/Economics

By now it should be apparent that regenerating and growing white pine is not easy—nor is it inexpensive. Undoubtedly, these factors are some of the reasons why so little white pine has been planted. If we look at the costs alone, without fully understanding the economics of white pine, the picture is daunting. However, if we give white pine an economic value and project out its price with a 5 percent annual increase, the analysis looks much better.

First, some information on regeneration costs. No two sites are exactly alike so the costs of regenerating white pine will vary. Some areas will require more site preparation; others will have more competition; and others will simply cost more overall to plant. The following are averages for 200,000 trees planted on 200 acres of our sites during 1996 and 1997:

Prescription	Cost/1,000 seedlings	Cost per acre
Shelterwood harvest premium	none	none
Site preparation		$45.00
Herbicide		$55.00
Herbicide applicator		$35.00
Planting stock	$140.00	
Contract planting	$70.00	
Bud capping 5 cents/tree x 900 trees/acre x 5 years (200 earlier acres)	$250.00	$225.00
Hand release in 5th year as necessary (200 earlier acres)		$28.00

If we assume that 1,000 seedlings are planted per acre and 900 survive until the fifth year, we can translate these costs back and forth to establish total regeneration and early treatment costs of $645 per 1,000 seedlings, or $598 per acre.

This could be considered the worst case scenario. If the site is cleaner and has less competitive vegetation, or if there is less deer browsing, these costs can be substantially reduced. As earlier mentioned, picking the best sites and keeping growth/survival factors in mind is important. They will certainly have a major bearing on ultimate regeneration costs. For land managers with thousands of acres to choose from, picking economical sites is easy. For the landowner who has less acreage, regenerating white pine will require taking the steps that are necessary and paying the price.

It is not easy to calculate the absolute value of a forest. For each landowner it will be different, depending on what the forest represents to them. For some, the aesthetic or recreational values will be greater than to another landowner. The same is true for wildlife habitat or for numerous other values. There is one universal value, however, that is often asked about when talking about white pine: its value as timber stumpage for forest products. We are frequently asked, 'What is a tree "worth?"'

White pine ranks very high in value for softwood lumber and veneer. Much sought-after for its soft texture, stability, warm appearance and machinability, white pine could be considered our most valuable major species. Then, amplified by the fact that it is fast growing and the trees get large, white pine can substantially hold its own against the lower regeneration costs of other species. Consideration can also be given to the great opportunity to increase grade (quality) in white pine because its lower limbs can be readily pruned, thereby providing large, clear trunk logs (butt cuts).

It is not uncommon to yield 40,000 board feet per acre from stands over a period of 80 years. If the stand has been well-managed, the trees will yield stumpage values for lumber and veneer that, at 1997 prices, are $250 per thousand board feet (MBF). For the purpose of economic analysis (since rarely would anyone clearcut such a stand) this present day, $10,000 per acre yield would compare favorably with the cost of raising the stand.

A simple way of calculating this is to say that money's worth (un-compounded) doubles every 10 years. If we take the $600 per acre cost and double it again and again, eight times, the result is $153,600. Now, go back and double the stumpage value four times (reflecting the historic 5 percent annual increase in stumpage prices multiplied times 80 years), and the calculated stumpage value is $160,000. As surprising as these calculations might first appear, working backwards 80 years to 1917 would indicate that the stumpage price was $15/MBF and regeneration cost was $2/acre. This is certainly realistic.

A major criticism and what the general public is encouraged to believe by preservationist leaders and major media is that Minnesota forests are being destructively clear-cut and turned into aspen monocultures—all to feed pulp mills and waferboard plants. It simply is not so.

There is a substantial—albeit private and quiet—lumber industry in this state that promotes the growth of big trees from high quality forests. Over 200 independent sawmills scattered amongst small towns in Minnesota produce over 300,000,000 board feet of lumber each year for home builders, furniture/millwork/cabinet shops, window/door manufacturers, and a whole host of other wonderful and important wood products. In terms of total employment, more people make their livelihoods in wood products such as these than do from pulp and paper. These smaller, independent sawmills desire well-developed stands of large trees as much as anyone, and probably do the most to promote the development of such stands.

The supply of Minnesota trees to sawmills is critical to sustain the availability of these important products and jobs. White pine is no longer the "King of the Forest" nor is it of lumber. But it is a very valuable and highly prized wood for lumber and veneer. It is only too bad there isn't more of it because it is likely the most valuable lumber tree in all the forest. Today we have the opportunity and responsibility to grow it for future generations—a time when it will be even more valuable.

It was sawmilling that *broke* white pine originally. It was cut hard without thought of regenerating it. The investment simply was not made. Paradoxically, it is the value of white pine lumber and veneer that will *make* white pine today and in the future. The tremendous effort and investment that is required is justified economically by what we can make today from these valuable trees. Just as it has been in New England, Michigan, and Wisconsin, it is now the market (the sawmill, so to say) that will offer the price for bringing back the white pine.

SECTION
6

AUTHOR'S NOTES

EPILOGUE

AUTHOR'S NOTES

The Rajala Companies have planted approximately two million seedlings in the past 20 years. Our surveys show that we have one million, only one-half, still growing. Certainly, this is not good news. We made mistakes, many of them, as we tried to figure out how to grow white pine. Would we do it all over again? Of course we would. From the standpoint of what we have so laboriously learned we feel much more assured of success today.

The major mistakes have been these:

- We planted white pine in places where we shouldn't have. Trying to handle large sites where mesic and nutrient-rich soils brought fierce competitive vegetation—especially under too much canopy—was more of a challenge than we were prepared for.

- We did not properly set up many of the sites. We left too much (50 percent or more) upper canopy and did not take enough of the lower and intermediate canopy out. We have too many white pine seedlings starving for sunlight.

- We underestimated the challenge of competition from maple and hazel brush and did not adequately prevent its growth by using better site scarification or herbicide treatment.

- We seriously underestimated the challenges of preventing and the effects of deer browsing-especially when coupled with slow growth rates caused by poor stock (compounded by the mistakes mentioned above).

- Finally, and perhaps most importantly, we were guilty of "walk away forestry." Even though we knew regenerating white pine would be difficult and we visited our sites at least once a year, this was not enough. In the Minnesota forest, white pine needs help. This means watching the little trees carefully and then responding to each threat and impediment vigorously . . . whether this response is bud capping, releasing, pruning, or some other forest management tool.

A hard story. Tough lessons. But worth it. In those places where we did most things right (or even in places where we did only one thing right) we are experiencing a surprising amount of natural regeneration from native seed sources. So, there's a bonus, a reward for doing something.

This is a good place to draw it all together and conclude these writings. Some proponents of white pine believe the answer is to stay away from it and leave it alone; others believe that natural regeneration, with some help (like prescribed burning) is the answer. Others of us believe that the task of restoring white pine requires the additional effort of getting out there and planting and managing. It is doubtful there will ever be total agreement on this. The mystery of forests, and consequently, forestry, is just that way.

My journey with white pine has been a long one. It is a tree that is so near and dear to my heart that I still stand in awe as I study these trees—large and small alike. But the time has come for me to see many other things in the forest as well.

I have turned my focus to growing and managing white birch. This species will likely be as challenging and consuming as white pine. But I know that I will never, never lose my penchant for white pine. It is a passion many of us share.

During the past 1-1/2 years while this book was being written, the interest and controversy surrounding white pine has continued to expand. White pine has dominated the coverage of forestry issues in all of the television, radio, newspaper, and magazine media in Minnesota during 1996 and 1997.

In March 1996, a coalition of preservationist groups sponsored a bill that was authored and heard by Willard Munger in the Minnesota Legislature House of Representatives-Environment and Natural Resources Committee. It called for a moratorium on the harvesting of white pine on state lands. No hearings were held on the Senate side so the bill was dropped.

One of the major accusations made by sponsors of the moratorium was that very little, if any, work was being done to regenerate or manage white pine in Minnesota. Therefore, the bill's sponsors argued, future harvesting of white pine should be banned until the State of Minnesota had a program to protect and manage the species and until there was full monitoring of management accomplishments.

Another indictment promulgated by the bill's sponsors was that only 1 to 2 percent of the forest acres that had white pine during pre-settlement time had white pine now. It was further asserted that the acres of white pine cover type today equaled only 63,000 acres and that this figure has declined during the past 15 years.

I, along with other land managers, conducted a survey to test the validity of these assertions and to gain knowledge of white pine management throughout the state. Even though several large forest products companies with forested land and several counties with commercial forest land did not supply data, it was learned that Minnesota has at least 85,000 acres of white pine cover type, and that age-class is fairly well distributed.

The survey revealed two other very important facts: First, there are over 100,000 acres in Minnesota where there are five white pine trees or more per acre, and over 1 million acres that have at least one white pine tree per acre. Secondly, there was unanimously high interest by all respondents in growing more white pine. However, most land managers were seeking methodology and adequate budgets before putting white pine regeneration and management "into gear."

Undoubtedly in response to the legislative activity to consider the banning of harvesting white pine, the Commissioner of the Minnesota Department of Natural Resources established the White Pine Regeneration Strategies Work Group in April 1996. This committee of 16 experts was asked to develop recommendations for the regeneration and management of white pine on state lands and to report to the Commissioner by December 1996.

The group, chaired by Bruce Zumbahlen of the DNR and Craig Locey of the U.S. Forest Service, thoroughly studied pre-settlement white pine data, forest succession, ecological classification data and systems, and current forest management practices. The group took testimony from ecologists, silviculturists, researchers, and land managers, as well as the general public.

In presenting its final report in December 1996, the White Pine Strategies Work Group made recommendations in five general categories. The expectation was that these recommendations, if heeded, would significantly increase the presence of white pine in Minnesota. The five categories are:

1. Planning/Budgeting

2. Management/Regeneration

3. Education/Training

4. Research

5. Inventory/Monitoring

Even though the group's report was widely heralded as the finest compendium of state-of-the-art thinking and recommendations to increase white pine in Minnesota, another coalition of preservationist groups again called for a bill to ban the harvest of white pine during the 1997 legislative session. However, although there was buzzing about such a moratorium in the corridors of the Capitol, no hearings were held and no bill came forth.

Instead, a preservationist coalition put severe pressure on the commissioner of the DNR to have the DNR totally redesign its forest management and timber sale planning process, and called for wide-open public participation and appeal mechanisms in that process.

In May 1997, the Commissioner appointed a committee representing a full cross-section of interests in white pine. The committee's charge was to make recommendations about how to "increase public participation in the DNR planning process for white pine." After five full days of meetings, consensus was reached by the group and recommendations to significantly and effectively change planning were reported to the Commissioner.

It should be noted that even after participating in the consensus process, the activist group Earth First released to the media a press release that stated the recommendations were a sham.

SECTION
7

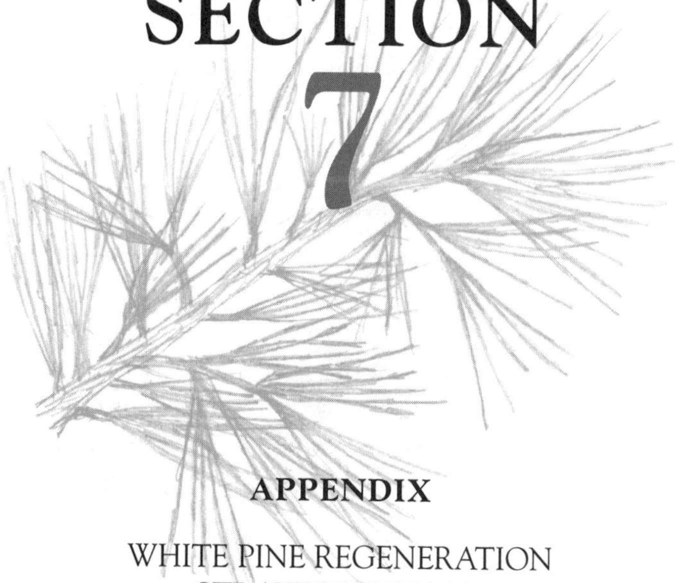

APPENDIX

WHITE PINE REGENERATION
STRATEGIES WORK
GROUP REPORT

SILVICULTURAL SYSTEMS

REFERENCES

BIBLIOGRAPHY

APPENDIX

WHITE PINE REGENERATION STRATEGIES WORK GROUP REPORT

⫸Introduction

White pine is a focus of attention in Minnesota's forests. It stands as a reminder not only of times gone by, but also as an indicator of the present and a promise for the future. Its contributions are many: nesting habitats for birds of prey and cavity dwellers; safe havens for some wildlife; valuable wood for a growing population; beauty; and playing a role in the forest ecosystem that we may never completely understand. All these contributions are critical, and all of them must be sustained.

For myriad reasons there are not as many white pine trees in Minnesota's forests as most people would like. The reasons include substantial harvesting for lumber in the late 1800s and early 1900s; clearing of forested land for agricultural, urban, highway, utility, and other uses; the introduction of blister rust from Europe; a greatly increased deer population that often feeds on white pine; and emphasis on the management of tree species other than white pine.

In response to widespread concern about the white pine resource in Minnesota, a White Pine Regeneration

Strategies Work Group was appointed in early 1996 by the Minnesota Department of Natural Resources. The specific mission of the Work Group was to prepare a report for the Minnesota Forest Resources Council containing the following information:

- The status of Minnesota's white pine resource and its historical and current occurrence.

- Existing efforts to increase the white pine resource through management strategies and practices.

- Research needed to address specific concerns about white pine where more knowledge is needed or where adequate data is lacking to conduct an analysis.

- Recommended regeneration and management strategies that would increase the role and presence of white pine.

The Work Group believes the role and presence of white pine in Minnesota should be increased significantly, both in the short term and the long term. To do so will require the combined efforts of all stakeholders in Minnesota. Specifically, the Work Group recommends the following goals be adopted:

1. Appropriate silvicultural systems, including long term monitoring and care, should be used to ensure retention and regeneration of white pine on suitable sites throughout its pre-European settlement range in Minnesota.

2. The number of white pine trees and the number of acres of young white pine trees should be doubled within the next seven years. The number of acres in white pine cover type should be doubled within the next 50 years.

3. Over the long term, management activities should increase the acreage and spatial dispersion of older white pine stands. They should also create an age distribution of white pine stands that is more balanced than the current distribution.

4. Harvesting activities should be planned and conducted within the context of silvicultural systems designed to increase the growth and/or regeneration of white pine.

5. Critical research in the areas of deer predation, regeneration systems, genetic improvement, and blister rust management should be conducted and reported as quickly as possible.

6. Educational materials and programs that explain and promote white pine management should be developed and distributed to resource managers and private landowners.

7. Site level ecological classification systems should be completed because of their usefulness in identifying suitable white pine sites.

8. Best Management Practices (BMP)-type audits should be used to evaluate the success of specific regeneration activities. Forest Inventory Analysis data should

be used to evaluate the accomplishment of goals related to the abundance, age distribution, and spatial dispersion of white pine.

9. Budgeting and funding decisions should support activities that help accomplish the goals stated above.

The means for accomplishing these goals are contained in the recommendations listed in the following section. The recommendations were developed by the Work Group with input from members of the White Pine Review/Advisory Group. They were included using a consensus approach; only if all members of the Work Group agreed were they included.

Recommendations are grouped in five categories: Planning/Budgeting, Management/Regeneration, Education/Training, Research, and Inventory/Monitoring. For each recommendation, a brief explanation of why the recommendation was made is provided. While varying in scope, the Work Group believes each of the recommended actions will have a positive impact on the white pine resource in Minnesota.

The basis for all the recommendations is information about the history, status, ecology, pests, and management of white pine the Work Group gathered through a series of meetings and field trips, including a meeting with members of the White Pine Review/Advisory Group.

⇗Recommendations

Planning/Budgeting

Sites where white pine occurred prior to European settlement are now owned by private individuals and companies, counties, state and federal agencies, and tribal
governments. Because of differences in site characteristics, management opportunities for white pine are much
better on some classes of land ownership than on others.
Planning and funding decisions should recognize the dif-
fering opportunities for white pine management within
and among ownerships, and target the opportunities and
activities which are likely to have the most success. The
recommendations in this section provide basic guidelines regarding planning and budgeting decisions that
will be necessary to significantly increase the presence
and role of white pine in Minnesota.

1. Recommendation:

Set a regeneration goal so that the acreage of white
pine stocked with 25 or more trees per acre under 5
inches (dbh) will be doubled from 149,000 acres to
298,000 acres over the next seven years through a
combination of fostering natural regeneration and
planting. In both natural regeneration and planting
systems, there should be appropriate measures to
promote growth and protection from pathogens and
wildlife browsing for the early critical years.

Explanation/Rationale:

The 1990 Minnesota Forest Inventory and Analysis
(FIA) shows that there are 149,000 acres that have
25 or more white pine trees less than 5 inches dbh.
A seven year period would enable forest land man-

agement agencies to expand their white pine regeneration capabilities; this period of time would also coincide with the publication of the second 5-year statewide forest reinventory report that could be used to track progress towards the goal.

2. Recommendation:

Through the budgeting process, public funding should:

1: Target silviculture efforts that favor the survival and development of existing white pine regeneration;

2: Target silvicultural methods that favor establishment of natural regeneration;

3: Target planting, especially in areas with little or no existing white pine.

Explanation/Rationale:

The survival of much of the existing white pine regeneration is dependent on release efforts. This would be one of the most effective means to increase white pine in Minnesota. It is also important to modify harvesting techniques and to utilize site preparation to encourage natural white pine regeneration. Planting efforts will be needed in most cases to increase the acreage of white pine.

3. Recommendation

Each DNR forestry area, state park, major wildlife management unit, and county land department within the range of white pine should set targets to increase the presence of white pine on lands under their administration through a process that incorporates goals set forth in this report.

Explanation/Rationale:
Goals established through a planning process based on stand level data are more achievable than arbitrary goals established without the expertise and input from local resource managers and key stakeholder groups. Given the training to identify suitable sites for white pine management and the resources to implement their plans, resource managers would be more effective in attaining the goals.

4. Recommendation:
The Department of Natural Resources (DNR) should develop a state-funded incentives program to encourage the establishment and long-term management of white pine on non-industrial private forest (NIPF) lands. This state-funded incentive program should be developed in coordination with the Forest Stewardship Program, and be implemented through Forest Stewardship Plans and Stewardship Incentives Program practices.

Explanation/Rationale:
Private individuals own about 40% of the land occupied by the white pine type in Minnesota and about 50% of the land in areas where white pine occurred prior to European settlement. With such large ownerships, private individuals can play a significant role in regenerating and managing white pine. An incentive program will encourage these landowners to make the extra effort necessary to grow white pine.

5. Recommendation:

Forest land management organizations should plan harvest schedules or other disturbance regimes and time the establishment of new areas of white pine cover type so that age classes of the white pine resource are distributed more evenly.

Explanation/Rationale

An even distribution of stand ages within each landscape region of the state would help ensure that stands of various ages would always be present, thus benefitting the maintenance of biodiversity and help to insure a steady flow of white pine timber in the future.

6. Recommendation:

Funding should be made available to county land management organizations actively encouraging the establishment and long-term management of white pine on county-administered lands.

Explanation/Rationale:

County-administered lands represent approximately 18% of the sites containing white pine at the time of the public land survey. As such, they represent a significant opportunity for increasing the role and presence of white pine in Minnesota. Those counties that demonstrate a commitment to establishing and managing white pine (e.g. development and use of white pine management guidelines) should be recognized and receive priority in the allocation of funds made available through white pine budget initiatives.

7. Recommendation:

An advocate for white pine regeneration should be a participant at DNR goal setting processes designed to set the deer population goal in areas where increased regeneration is desirable.

Explanation/Rationale:

Deer management in Minnesota is predicated on a system of "population goals" and antlerless permits are adjusted on an annual basis to maintain deer density near these goals. Some sort of "round table" process will be used within the next year to revise these goals. Typically, participants are invited to attend these meetings to review the consequences of changes to deer density, "reflect" their concerns and attempt to reach consensus on whether to change population goals. These meetings will represent the primary opportunity for all stakeholders to discuss how deer numbers should be managed. As importantly, the goals set at these meetings will form the basis for subsequent management.

Recommendations

Management/Regeneration

The ecology of white pine is different from most other conifers in Minnesota. To successfully regenerate and manage it, activities not normally used for other species will be necessary (e.g., under planting, protection from deer browse, pruning). In addition to increasing the number of white pine trees, there is also the need to increase spatial dispersion, increase the number of old trees and stands, and smooth out the age distribution. Accomplishing these goals will require significant regeneration efforts, modified silvicultural systems, long term care, and some harvesting limitations, as described in the following recommendations.

1. Recommendation:

Harvests of white pine in the pine cover types on state-administered land should be restricted to thinnings, selective harvests, or shelterwood harvests. When harvesting white pine in other forest cover types, the best seed producing white pine will be retained and treatments carried out so as to increase white pine regeneration. These restrictions shall govern planning and timber sale design by managers on state-administered lands until new inventory indicates that the number of white pine trees has doubled from 25.9 to 51.8 million trees on all ownerships. An exception to these restrictions would allow harvest if a tree poses a hazard to the public or has been severely damaged by natural causes.

Explanation/Rationale:

Thinnings and selective harvest enables the capture of mortality before it occurs (e.g. extensive blister rust) and allows the remaining trees to grow bigger, faster. Shelterwood harvests are a proven silvicultural system that fosters regeneration of white pine. Leaving good seed producing trees in other types would provide a seed source for expanding the presence of white pine.

2. Recommendation:

Forest land management organizations should be encouraged to reserve the better white pine trees that occur as scattered individuals or in small groups for their seed producing, aesthetic, wildlife, and ecological benefits.

Explanation/Rationale:

One of the factors contributing to the decline of white pine in Minnesota is the absence of seed producing trees for natural regeneration. Reserving groups of mature trees may preserve genetic characteristics that will allow white pine to continue adapting to changes in climate, predation pressure and diseases. These trees have value as a source of seed if steps are taken to encourage natural regeneration around them. They also have value for aesthetics, ecological, and wildlife purposes even if they are dead or dying since they can serve as excellent nesting, roosting, and snag trees.

3. Recommendation:

All white pine on state-administered timber land should be managed under the DNR's Extended Rotation Forest (ERF) Guideline so as to increase the acreage and distribution of older white pine stands and trees on the landscape.

Explanation/Rationale:

The total acreage of older white pine existing on public lands today is much less than what existed prior to European settlement. Managing all white pine on state-administered timber lands to attain ERF final harvest ages of 150-180 years would help to restore the ecological values associated with older white pine trees and stands while providing a long-term seed source for establishing white pine regeneration.

4. Recommendation:

White pine should be planted in smaller groups as well as on larger acreages within its range where white pine was once abundant but is now rare or non-existent.

Explanation/rationale:

White pine was historically and is today more commonly found as a component of other forest types rather than as a pure white pine forest type. In order to re-establish its former role, it is important to establish a presence on favorable sites throughout its range, whether as larger stands or as more scattered individuals and groups. Planting of small groups of white pine on appropriate sites can be incorporated into reforestation programs for other species so that white pine is established as a component of the new stand.

5. Recommendation:

Managers should enhance natural seeding opportunities through treatments that create proper microsites for seedling establishment near white pine seed trees when natural and man-made disturbances occur. Treatments in the vicinity of seed trees could include mechanical scarification, prescribed burns, or leaving or enhancing the presence of coarse woody debris in advanced stages of decay on the forest floor.

Explanation/Rationale:

Natural seeding can be effective aesthetically and economically. Harvesting, windthrow, wildfire, and insect outbreaks can create openings around seed-bearing white pine trees where regeneration could be attempted or facilitated with minimal effort (e.g. use of scarification). Recognition of these opportunities and efforts to take advantage of these should result in substantial increases in white pine regeneration.

6. Recommendation:

The DNR should create a forum for resource managers that manage areas reserved from harvest for the purpose of identifying and discussing management techniques, including intensive management practices, to assist in the establishment, regeneration and maintenance of white pine in reserved areas.

Explanation/Rationale:

Managers of reserved areas (e.g.: parks, Scientific and Natural Areas, designated old-growth stands) need a set of techniques that they can use to maintain or increase the amount of white pine when that is identified as a management objective. Reserved areas often have as an overarching management goal the use and maintenance of natural processes: traditional silvicultural practices are often not used because they alter natural processes. On the other hand, the processes and disturbances that created the white pine stands that exist today may not function the way they did before settlement, or they may be unavailable as management tools. Management techniques that use or mimic natural processes and can be practically applied in the field are required.

7. Recommendation:

DNR tree nurseries should expand the procurement of white pine seed native to Minnesota in collaboration with other forest land management agencies and work with private nurseries to grow more white pine adapted to Minnesota's conditions.

Explanation/Rationale:

Native seed sources should be used to ensure adequate survival and growth of planted seedlings adapted to Minnesota conditions. In order to expand the amount of white pine planting stock, more aggressive seed collection and procurement strategies need to be in place to capture good seed crops in the different seed zones. At some point, seed orchards should provide a large amount of the white pine seed needed.

8. Recommendation:

The DNR should protect (maintain) selected stands of white pine greater than 20 acres in size in various age classes on state-administered lands to provide for future old growth. Limited harvesting for sanitation and maintenance may be allowed in some of the selected stands to help perpetuate the life of the stand and promote regeneration. Resource managers on federal and county-administered lands are encouraged to also follow this recommendation.

Explanation/Rationale:

The ecological values associated with old growth are more likely to be found in stands greater than 20 acres. This will ensure that old-growth stands will occur in the future.

9. Recommendation:

The DNR should protect (maintain) older white

pine stands greater than 20 acres in size so that approximately 25 percent of the acreage of these older and larger stands exceeds 120 years of age on state-administered lands. Fifty percent of the acreage of these stands older than 120 years should be maintained as old growth. Resource managers on federal and county-administered lands are encouraged to also follow this recommendation.

Explanation/Rationale:

The total acreage of this age and stand size on public lands today is probably less than 5 percent of what existed in Minnesota prior to European settlement. A significant amount of what remains should be maintained for scientific research, aesthetic, and recreational purposes.

10. Recommendation:

The Commissioner of Natural Resources, in cooperation with stakeholders should create a pilot project to identify blocks of state lands in management units of the Outdoor Recreation Act (e.g. state forest, state park) where deer density would be reduced for the short term (5-7 years) to allow white pine regeneration to out-grow the reach of the deer.

Explanation/Rationale:

It is well accepted that deer browse white pine during the winter and can retard or prevent successful regeneration. It is not clear however, whether regeneration can be stimulated by simply reducing local deer numbers. There are at least 3 advantages to using this approach. First, fewer hunters would be impacted if only specific blocks are targeted rather than entire Deer Management Areas. Second, the proposal is short term and affects deer numbers only during a specific "window" when the primary goal would be to increase white pine regeneration. third, the blocks represent an opportunity to test whether sufficient cooperation from hunters can be secured to reduce deer number effectively and whether reduced deer numbers measurably affects regeneration.

11. Recommendation:
Resource managers should increase the use of prescribed surface fires to regenerate white pine on reserved and commercial forest land.

Explanation/Rationale:
It is known that historically white pine was established in pure and mixed stands by surface fires and crown fires. With fire suppression, shade-tolerant trees and shrubs are increasing throughout the white pine's range. Mature white pine stands especially need surface fires, or "underburning", to establish new cohorts of pines. The known benefits of using fire include reducing brush in the forest understory, reducing the duff layer to expose a mineral seed bed, and reducing the fire hazard, and other unknown benefits may also exist.

12. Recommendation:
The Minnesota Conservation Corps (MCC) should be utilized as a partner in conducting management activities that will promote the presence of white pine. For the next few years, a significant portion of the MCC's time should be devoted to projects

directly related to increasing the presence of white pine on the landscape.

Explanation/Rationale:

The MCC provides an existing workforce that would be readily available to land managers for conducting projects beneficial to white pine. Examples of projects might include: pruning to reduce blister rust infection; planting; release of seedlings and saplings from competition; and bud-capping young trees to protect them from deer.

➤ Recommendations

Education/Training

Much is known about regenerating and managing white pine, but not all of it is readily available to landowners and resource managers. The recommendations in this section are aimed at increasing the dissemination of useful information to private individuals, forest land managers, and others directly responsible for or interested in white pine management in the state.

1. Recommendation:

A "Silvicultural Guide" should be developed to recommend the care and management of white pine.

Guidelines should address the variety of landowners and land classifications in Minnesota (e.g. parks; natural areas; private, county, state, and federal ownerships). The following must be included in this guide:

- Focus and emphasis should be placed on the importance of care and management practices of white pine after regeneration and establishment. Follow-up practices ensuring the establishment of seedlings by release from competing vegetation should be suggested.

- Emphasis must be placed on the range of difficulty of establishing white pine from one type of site to another; information must be given on what pre-scriptions are necessary on each site.

- Additional management options, site analysis considerations, and cultural practices should be included.

Explanation/Rationale:

"State-of-the-art" recommendations on white pine regeneration and management should be available to all landowners in the State of Minnesota. The range of ease/difficulty with the regeneration and management of white pine from one type of site to another should be addressed and information provided on appropriate prescriptions for each type of site.

It is essential that public and private individuals and agencies recognize the need for timber stand improvement (TSI) practices after regeneration and establishment. These TSI techniques might include, but are not limited to pathological pruning and release work.

Walk-away forestry will not suffice for the regeneration and establishment of white pine in Minnesota.

2. Recommendation:

Develop a continuing education program for foresters that explains and demonstrates management techniques that can increase the presence of white pine. This program needs to teach how to take advantage of, and enhance natural regeneration opportunities as well as incorporate artificial processes (e.g. site preparation work, prescribed burns, planting). A similar program should also be available to all forest landowner groups and timber harvesters. These programs should consider the development of areas that demonstrate regeneration and management techniques.

Explanation/Rationale:

There is a good deal of skepticism about managing white pine and uncertainty about how to do it. Education needs to be directed toward hands-on learning and the building of networks among managers so they can communicate with one another about problems and successes.

3. Recommendation:

Educational materials should be developed for non-industrial private forest landowners that describe white pine ecology, values, and silviculture, and that encourage landowners to regenerate and manage white pine on appropriate sites. These materials should reveal the numerous opportunities and scientific data available to make white pine regeneration a success. These materials should emphasize that the success will depend on commitment and follow-up treatments. There should be active promotion for white pine management in "stewardship plans" on appropriate sites.

Explanation/Rationale:

Existing literature stresses white pine problems rather than balancing the values of white pine with management considerations. Significant gains can be made if people are provided with a "recipe for success." No such educational materials are currently available.

4. Recommendations:

The DNR should prepare a brief key that can be used by resource managers to identify potential sites for white pine management that currently lack a white pine component.

Explanation/Rationale:

A key that describes common plant associations of white pine along with soil moisture and nutrient characteristics required by white pine would serve as a useful tool to resource managers in identifying sites suitable for white pine management.

5. Recommendation:

Establish an "Adopt Young White Pines" program that provides education, training, and recognition to any individual, family, or organized group that adopts a young white pine site managed by participating public forest land management agencies and that agrees to apply cultural practices that will protect young white pine from pest problems during their early critical years.

Explanation/Rationale:

White pine are most vulnerable to damage from blister rust, deer browsing, and tip weevil when they are young. Pruning the lower branches and bud capping until the seedling is above browse height are two practices that would increase their potential for survival. This could be accomplished through the dedicated care of an individual or organization that has indicated a commitment by enrolling in a program such as Adopt Young White Pines.

⚡Recommendations

Inventory/Monitoring
Good decisions about the regeneration and management of white pine on specific sites requires useful information about the site. Site classification systems provide such information more accurately than simply using the existing cover type. This section recommends that site classification systems be developed for Minnesota because of their potential value in selecting appropriate sites on which to regenerate and manage white pine. It also recommends that monitoring systems be developed to measure the effectiveness of white pine management activities, and changes in the overall status of the white pine resources.

1. Recommendation:
Forest land management organizations should develop ecological classification systems that have utility for managing white pine at the field level and that address plant community dynamics.

Explanation/Rationale:
Thoughtful forest management requires information on the ecological potential of a site; cover types are not enough. An ecological classification system that

places sites in an ecological context and offers potential successional pathways will be of great utility. As a tool for land managers, it will:

- Identify potential sites for white pine management that are currently without a white pine component.
- Determine degree of difficulty in establishing white pine and the type of silvicultural system most likely to succeed.
- Help identify pest problems related to a specific site.
- Look beyond present cover type and recognize ecological potential of a site to support cover types in addition to the present cover type.
- Provide common site interpretive language for resource managers of various resource specialties.
- Serve as a tool in future forest inventories to help predict future forest cover type trends and potential site opportunities to meet future management objectives.

2. Recommendation:

The Department of Natural Resources should develop a comprehensive monitoring program to evaluate the effectiveness of managing for white pine at the stand level. The program should be designed to select relevant sites through a stratified random sampling process. It should also include field audits similar to those used in the Best Management Practices to Protect Water Quality program.

Explanation/Rationale:

Follow-up monitoring and evaluation are essential to

the success of establishing white pine regeneration and management for white pine. Monitoring the tending needs beyond initial regeneration surveys is essential to protecting and enhancing previous investments and ensuring success. Silvicultural recommendations for white pine management prepared by the White Pine Regeneration Strategies Work Group could be used in the evaluation in the absence of specific guidelines. Including stakeholders in the field audits would build creditability to the process. A "walk away" mentality after initial establishment must be discouraged.

3. Recommendation:

The Annual Forest Inventory System (AFIS) should be used to the extent possible in assessing the condition of the white pine resource and monitoring progress towards goals.

Explanation/Rationale:

The Forest Inventory Analysis (FIA) is managed by the U.S. Forest Service's research stations to periodically inventory the state's forests. The DNR cooperates on conducting FIA in Minnesota and has been working with the U.S. Forest Service on a pilot project, the Annual Forest Inventory System (AFIS), to provide more frequent updates on the condition of the state's forests. AFIS has been designed to provide a complete statewide reinventory every 4 years along with a continuously updated data base kept current through annual field sampling, use of satellite imagery, and computer modeling.

⚹ Recommendations

Research

Although much is known about white pine, there are some critical gaps in the knowledge base. Major areas needing additional research include deer predation, blister rust management, white pine genetics, natural regeneration techniques, old growth systems, and the costs and benefits of growing white pine. The following recommendations identify research which should be conducted to assist white pine management efforts.

1. Recommendation:

Research should be funded to address the following questions concerning white-tailed deer:

1. Determine the extent of deer browsing that will kill or retard seedling growth enough that it will lose its competitive edge.
2. Determine whether there is a threshold in patch/plantation size and/or seedling densities at which deer browsing will not prevent sufficient stocking levels to occur.
3. Determine whether there are specific "habitat types" in which white pine is less likely to be browsed.
4. Determine deer palatability as it relates to seed source and type of planting stock.

Explanation/Rationale:

It is well documented that deer browse white pine seedlings, but it is not clear how severe this browsing must be to kill an individual tree. It is well-known that many animals produce so many young that predators are overwhelmed, and sufficient numbers of young survive to be recruited to an adult population. A likely parallel may be applied to white pine seedlings covering the landscape in fairly large batches. This begs the question: Can larger areas or high densities of seedlings be planted to "overwhelm" browsing by deer?

Deer browse white pine primarily in winter on their winter range. Assuming a classification scheme is identified for determining where white pine should be planted, is it possible to identify specific "habitat types" that represent winter habitat or yarding areas of deer, thus areas of potential high browsing of white pine?

2. Recommendation:
Research efforts should be funded to refine management and harvesting practices that improves the cost effectiveness of regeneration, and expansion of white pine from individual trees, clusters or stands.

Explanation/Rationale:
Additional information is needed to develop reliable practices for regenerating clumps or small stands of white pine. Information is also needed on how to promote regeneration around isolated trees and how to expand clumps or small stands beyond their current size.

3. Recommendation:
Research should be funded to address the following concerns with blister rust in the State of Minnesota.

- Investigate methods of predicting site specific blister rust impacts: Where will severe impacts be likely and, therefore, where will management of white pine be difficult.
- Develop management tools and techniques that can be utilized in Minnesota to reduce the impact of blister rust.

Explanation/Rationale:

Almost the entire northern 1/3 of Minnesota is within the two highest hazard zones for blister rust. However, field observation indicates that the levels of blister rust varies within that large area. If managers can predict where rust incidence will be great, or vice versa, successful regeneration efforts should be more likely.

White pine was originally distributed widely in the area now considered high hazard. Its re-establishment in those areas is desired. Therefore, management techniques that can be used to successfully regenerate white pine and reduce the impact of blister rust are highly desirable.

4. Recommendation:

Funding should be provided to develop genetic improvement in growth rates and blister rust resistance in white pine.

Explanation/Rationale:

Fast growing seedlings have several advantages. In an understory situation they may be able to compensate somewhat for the loss of growth normally associated with partial shade. They are likely to grow beyond deer browse and rust problems sooner. Grown in the right conditions, trees will become larger faster. Resistance to blister rust is polygenic (controlled by multiple genes) and several generations of breeding are necessary to fix resistance at a practical level. Polygenic resistance normally does not give complete protection (immunity), but the resistance is more permanent from generation to generation and should be more difficult for new races of blister rust to overcome.

5. Recommendation:

Research should be funded to study the regeneration processes that occur in old growth stands (as defined by the Minnesota Department of Natural Resources) where white pine is an important component.

Explanation/Rationale:

Old-growth stands are recognized as laboratories where the natural processes that have regenerated white pine for thousands of years can still be reconstructed. Most of what we know about natural processes in white pine stands has come from, and will continue to come from the few remnant stands in the state. Thus, knowledge about regeneration depends upon information obtained from these stands. The old-growth system and reserved lands in the Boundary Waters Canoe Area Wilderness, Scientific and Natural Areas, Research Natural Areas, state parks, or wherever old-growth stands occur can serve as these laboratories.

6. Recommendation:

An economic analysis should be conducted to gauge the potential benefit of intensively managing white pine under three situations: white pine stands, white pine as a component of other forest types, and where white pine is currently not present. The analysis should take into account different risk factors (e.g. blister rust hazard zones) and include costs associated with the long-term care required to grow white pine.

Explanation/Rationale:
Such an analysis will make it easier to justify the benefits of the intensive management and investment costs of white pine. Foresters, legislators, and the general public need to see that investment in white pine can be justified in economic terms as well as ecological terms.

White Pine Silvicultural Recommendations

General Considerations
White pine is a long-lived, disturbance-oriented species. In natural regimes these attributes affiliate white pine regeneration with fire and wind. White pine is moderately shade tolerant which enables it to become established in understories. White pine's ability to become established in understories reduces the impact of two pests: white pine tip weevil and blister rust.

White pine reaches the western edge of its natural range in Minnesota. Any plant on the edge of its natural range is going to encounter a higher percentage of its life span under some level of stress, compared to one growing in optimum conditions of its range. This contributes to periods of inconsistent regeneration and responses to management effort. Silvicultural systems developed in other areas of the eastern white pine range may need adjustments to be effective in Minnesota white pine ecosystems.

White pine rarely occurs in pure stands, but frequently occurs in mixture with other species. According to the 1990 forest inventory, 27 percent of the white pine volume occurs in stands where white pine makes up a plurality of the stand, while 73 percent of the volume occurs in other forest cover types. There are, of course, many sites where white pine once grew but is no longer present. In order to increase the presence and role of white pine, silvicultural systems must be adapted to each of these generalized situations:

- no white pine present
- white pine present as a minor species
- white pine present as a major species

White pine grows, or can grow, on a broad range of sites in Minnesota. This broad range of sites causes the character of stands containing white pine to vary from one part of the state to another. Ecological classification systems are new tools that can help sort out some of this variability and provide a means to recognize potential management options. These tools need to be developed down to the site level to be of full value to resource managers as they develop regeneration and management prescriptions.

Ecological classification systems will help synthesize and identify site characteristics that are important to growing white pine. These characteristics include soils, macro and micro climate, existing vegetation, potential competing vegetation, potential pest problems such as blister rust, and others. Using this information and landowner's goals, resource mangers can help identify management objectives and appropriate silvicultural systems for each site to foster the desired future species mixes.

In the case of white pine, success will be measured against the desired outcome (or management objective). In places where there is currently no white pine, the objective may simply be establishment of a few trees or groups of trees. Where a few white pine already exist, the objective might be to increase their number so they represent a plurality in the stand. Where white pine is already a plurality, the objective might be to maintain, and perhaps expand the stand.

There is no one "best" solution or prescription to increase white pine in Minnesota. Instead, there are multiple options for accomplishing this, driven by the site's ecological potential, stage of successional development, and the landowner's goals. The significant change in the analysis process is the determination of the site's ecological potential as compared to the traditional analysis of the present cover type. Identifying ecological potential should improve resource managers' success ratio and the ability to synthesize management recommendations at the landscape level.

White Pine Management Site Priority Considerations

- Identify ECS Subsections of the state where white pine was significant in the past and shows promise of response to management efforts.

- Within ECS Subsections, the following considerations at the site level seem a logical priority to consider:

  1. Sites where white pine reproduction already exists and can be enhanced through management.

  2. Sites where natural regeneration can be established through management.

  3. Sites where white pine regeneration will have to be established through planting.

Silvicultural Systems

Silvicultural systems are designed to prepare the site for regeneration of the next stand in addition to the harvest of products. The desired future species, or mix of species should be defined in the management unit (or stand) objective before harvest begins. Silvicultural systems describe how the harvest should be accomplished to prepare the site for regeneration.

Potential pest problems such as blister rust and tip weevil must be taken into account when developing a specific prescription for a silvicultural system to minimize pest problems.

Considering white pine biology, site selection priorities, and stand characteristics, the following silvicultural systems or combinations of them are viable considerations for white pine in Minnesota. On going and future Minnesota white pine research results will contribute to the refinement of these systems to conditions that exist in Minnesota. Since there are many combinations and variations of these systems, based on the conditions described earlier, the following systems will be described in general terms and would be more specific on a site-by-site basis.

White pine shelterwood method

The shelterwood system is flexible and provides time to evaluate results and make adjustments. While a shelterwood system offers significant flexibility, monitoring and follow up are imperative to ensure success. The follow-up period may extend 15 to 20 years beyond the initial harvest. The following steps describe a typical stand where there is sufficient white pine in the overstory to accomplish a shelterwood harvest and ensure natural regeneration.

1. At maturity, the stand canopy would be thinned to approximately 50 percent crown closure, allowing up to 50 percent of full sunlight to reach the forest floor. Suppressed and less desirable species would be removed in this harvest, leaving the more vigorous, desirable, seed-producing trees to provide a seed source and sufficient shade for germination and establishment of the next generation of seedlings.

2. After the first cut, the site should be left for at least two years to determine how intense sprout competition from other species will be and to allow slash to deteriorate. If the competition needs control, time the control with a good seed year and scarify as close to 80 percent of the site as possible. Since white pine is a disturbance-oriented species, and seeds germinate and establish themselves best on sites where the organic layer is lightly mixed with mineral soil, scarification is of the utmost importance. Prescribed fire is another site preparation alternative to scarification if conditions permit the use of fire.

3. Regeneration is considered successful when about 75 percent of the area is stocked with approximately 1,000 stems/acre. This reproduction may be a mixture of white pine and other desirable species associated with the particular type of site (or ecological unit).

4. Monitoring over a period of years should be done to determine if release will be necessary. After seedlings have become established, a second harvest cut may be initiated. This cut is intended to increase light and keep the seedlings growing vigorously. The second cut typically reduces the canopy closure to 20 percent, providing up to 80 percent of full sunlight. This also leaves enough seed-producing trees for insurance, should a failure occur.

5. Typically the final removal of the overstory and release of the new stand may be done over a period of years. Seldom is the regeneration uniform enough that a forest manager will want to release all of the stand at once.

*The system works well for the Menominee Tribal Enterprises in central Wisconsin.

These recommendations have been generalized; research and experience will fine-tune these recommendations for site conditions existing in Minnesota.

White pine seed tree method
When there are only a few scattered trees or clumps of white pine, then the seed tree method offers an opportunity to increase white pine through natural regeneration. Typically, these few white pine may be embedded in another cover type such as aspen or birch. In high blister rust hazard zones, a partial cut of the aspen/birch in the vicinity of the seed trees is recommended to serve the same purpose as a shelterwood. When the aspen or birch is harvested, the better seed producing white pine would be left. Within seed dispersal distance, seed bed preparation by scarification or prescribed fire, when appropriate, is imperative. The seed trees may be retained for an extended period of time if desirable. This system is ideally suited to increasing the white pine component in stands containing only scattered white pine. The seed tree system differs from the shelterwood system only in that fewer seed trees are present and the intermediate harvest to increase light is not needed.

White pine planting and seeding
On sites where there are few or no white pine present, and the ecological interpretation indicates it was once part of the system, planting is the most effective option. Planting white pine in the understory of another cover type can be successfully accomplished. Broadcast seeding

for white pine can also be done, but successful germination and survival of the seedlings is less assured.

The initial investment may be greater than natural regeneration because of the additional costs of site preparation, seedlings, planting, and control of competing vegetation. Like the other systems, monitoring over a period of years is imperative to successful establishment.

Planting may also be considered with shelterwood and seed tree systems to increase stocking if needed.

A) Planting under an existing overstory involves the following steps:

1. Thin the existing stand to a maximum of 70 percent crown closure, permitting at least 30 percent of full sunlight to reach the forest floor.

2. Prepare the site to expose mineral soil and control competing vegetation prior to planting.

3. If the object is to have white pine make up a plurality of the next stand, plant upwards of 1,000 seedlings per acre as uniformly spaced as possible. If the objective is to have white pine be a mixed component in the future stand, fewer seedlings per acre are needed. Planting small canopy gaps, particularly in high hazard blister rust areas, should be approached with caution. Dew often persists in these openings increasing the risk of blister rust infections on the newly planted seedlings.

4. Monitor over a period of years to determine if further release will be necessary.

5. Protect seedlings from browsing until they are five feet tall; prune lower branches of saplings to reduce the incidence of blister rust.

B) Planting in fields and openings can also be successful and will likely result in greater tree vigor. However, tree quality is often compromised by tip weevil damage, and the incidence of blister rust will likely increase.

Artificial seeding on sites that have been scarified is another technique that may be used when planting is too difficult. Like natural seeding, successful germination and survival are dependent on good seed bed conditions, and seed that has been stratified. If seeding is considered, it should be done in the fall to mimic natural conditions of seed dispersal.

It should be noted that the above recommendations are general in nature, but have been successfully implemented by both public and private landowners throughout Minnesota. Continuing research on white pine in Minnesota, documented field experience, and future research proposals, if approved, will be used to compile a comprehensive white pine silvicultural guide for Minnesota.

SILVICULTURAL SYSTEMS

Silvicultural systems and stand treatments commonly used in Minnesota:

Clearcut: Removal or felling, in a single cutting, of essentially all trees in the stand to prepare the site for natural or artificial regeneration of a new even-aged stand.

Clearcut with residual (reserves): A clearcutting method (as above) in which varying numbers of trees, or groups of trees, are not harvested to achieve a variety of objectives such as wildlife habitat improvement.

Group selection: A method of regenerating uneven aged stands in which trees are removed in small groups or patches and new age classes are established in the openings created. The maximum width of a group is approximately twice the average height of mature trees within the stand.

Patch clearcut: A clearcutting method (as above) in which the areas that are cut create an opening with a width greater than twice the height of a mature tree and which are less that 5 acres in size.

Seed tree: An even-aged regeneration method in which an area is clearcut except that certain trees, called seed trees, are left standing singly or in groups for the purpose of producing seed to restock the cleared area. Seed trees are removed after regeneration is established.

Shelterwood: A method of regenerating an even-aged stand by a series of partial cuttings, resembling thinnings, which extend over a small fraction of the life span of the stand. The residual canopy of mature trees provides protection and conditions for establishing new seedlings.

Single tree selection: A method of creating new age classes in uneven-aged stands in which individual trees of all size classes are removed more-or-less uniformly throughout the stands to achieve a desired stand structure.

Strip clearcut: A clearcutting method (as above) in which areas are cleared in strips. The residual strips are left as sources of seed for the cleared area.

Thinning: Commercial harvest of selected trees in a stand. Often the harvest trees are marked. Generally done to a) remove less desirable trees (species or form) from a stand; b) decrease stand density and increase future growth of remaining desirable trees.

Harvesting by silvicultural systems

A variety of silviculture systems and stand treatments are used in harvesting timber on forest lands. A silviculture system is a forest stand treatment designed to attain specific reforestation results. It is usually defined in terms of the harvest method used to prepare the site for reforestation. Some harvest methods (e.g. thinnings) are not intended to prepare a site for reforestation, but are designed to remove valuable products and improve the quality and growth potential of the remaining trees. These harvest methods are stand treatments, not silviculture systems.

A silviculture system or stand treatment is chosen for a site based on the desired tree species (or mix of species) being regenerated or the biological requirements of the stand being improved by a treatment. Some silviculture systems are more adapted to certain forest cover types than others. Management objectives for particular geographic areas along with application of suggested management guidelines also influence which silviculture system is prescribed to harvest timber.

⫸REFERENCES

Anderson, Ralph L., <u>A Summary of White pine Blister Rust in the Lake States</u>, USDA For. Ser. Res., North Cent. For. Exp. Stn., Note NC-6, St. Paul, MN, 1973.

Calvert, W.W. and L.G. Bruce, <u>Pruning and Sawing Eastern White Pine: A Case History From Stand Treatment to Utilization</u>, Canadian For. Serv., Petawawa For. Exp. Stn., Chalk River, Ont., 1965, 22p.

Frothingham, E.H., <u>White Pine Under Forest Management</u>, US Dept. of Ag., Bul. No. 13.

Katovich, Steven and Manfred Mielke, <u>How to Manage Eastern White Pine to Minimize Damage From Blister Rust and White Pine Weevil</u>, USDA For. Serv, NE Area State and Private Forestry, NA-FR-01-93, 1993, 14p.

Kittredge, David B. Jr., <u>Regenerating Eastern White Pine: Applying New and Old Knowledge</u>, Woodland Management Magazine, Oct. 1989, 4 p.

Lancaster, Kenneth F., <u>White Pine Management, A Quick Review</u>, USDA For. Serv., Northeastern For. Exp. Stn., S&PF, Res. Note NA-FR-27, Durham, NH, 1984, 4 p.

Lancaster, Kenneth F. and W.E. Leak, <u>A Silvicultural Guide for White Pine in the Northeast</u>, USDA For. Serv., NE For. Exp. Stn., Rep. NE-41, Broomall, PA, 1978, 13p.

Leatherby, Earl C. and John S. Spencer, Jr., Thomas L. Schmidt, Michael R. Carroll, <u>An Analysis of Minnesota's Fifth Forest Resources Inventory</u>, USDA For. Serv., North Cen. Exp. Stn., Res. Bul. NC0165, St. Paul, MN 1995, 102p.

<u>Minnesota's White Pine Now and For the Future: A Report by the White Pine Regeneration Strategies Work Group</u>, MN Dept. of Nat. Res. (Forestry), St. Paul, MN, 1996, 66p.

Page, Alan C. and David M. Smith, <u>Returns from Unrestricted Growth of Pruned Eastern White Pine</u>, Yale University School of Forestry, Bulletin No. 97, New Haven, CT, 1994.

<u>Proceedings of the White Pine Workshop</u>, USDA For. Ser., Chippewa Nat'l For., Cass Lake, MN, 1989, 81p.

Robbins, K., <u>How to Select Planting Sites for Eastern White Pine in the Lake States</u>, USDA For. Serv., NAFB/M-8, 1984.

Sauerman, Kurt, <u>Artificially Established White Pine Plantations in Minnesota: A Survey</u>, Unpublished, Univ. of MN Dept. of For. Res., Plan B Paper, St. Paul, MN, 1992.

Saunders, Mike and Klaus Puettman, <u>Effects of Herbivory and Competition on Growth of White Pine</u>, Unpublished, Univ. of MN Dept. of For. Res., St. Paul, MN, 1997, 4 p.

Smidt, Mathew and Klaus Puettman, <u>Understory and Canopy Competition Interact to Affect Growth of Underplanted White Pine in Minnesota</u>, Univ. of MN, Dept. of For. Res., St. Paul, MN 1996, 3p.

Van Arsdel, E.P., <u>Growing White Pine in the Lakes State to Avoid Blister Rust</u>, USDA For. Serv., Lake States For. Exp. Stn., Pap. 92, 1961, 11p.

<u>Some Forest Overstory Effects on Microclimate and Related White Pine Blister Rust Spread</u>, USDA For. Serv., Lake States For. Exp. Stn., Note 627, 1962.

Weber, Ray, <u>Early Pruning Reduces Blister Rust Mortality in White Pine Plantations</u>, USDA For. Serv., Lake States For. Exp. Stn., Res. Note LS-38, St. Paul, MN 1964, 2p.

<u>White Pine in Minnesota</u>, MN Dept. of Nat. Res. (Forestry), Study Report 1, 1992, 14p.

Wile, B.C., <u>Thinning in a White Pine Stand</u>, Canada Dept. of Northern Affairs and Natural Resources Tech. Note No. 5, 1955, 3 p.

Zasada, John C. and Glen W. Erickson, <u>Effect of Density on White Pine Stand Development in Northern Minnesota - A Case History</u>, Unpublished, North Cen. For. Exp. Stn. Grand Rapids, MN, 1996.

⇗BIBLIOGRAPHY

Frelich, Lee E., <u>The Relationship of Natural Disturbances to White Pine Stand Development: White PIne Symposium Proceedings</u>, Univ. of MN College of Nat. Res., St. Paul, MN, Sept. 1992.

Jacobson, George L., <u>A 7000 Year History of White Pine: White Pine Symposium Proceedings</u>, Univ. of MN College of Nat. Res., St. Paul, MN, Sept. 1992.

Krenz, Duane, "<u>Northern Timber" Range History</u>, Vol. 4, No. 2, June 1979.

Lancaster, K.F. and W.E. Leak, <u>A Silvicultural Guide for White Pine in the Northeast</u>, USDA For. Ser., NE For. Exp. Stn., Rep. NE-41, Broomall, PA, 1978.

Larson, Agnes M., <u>History of the White Pine Industry in Minnesota</u>, Univ. of MN Press, Mpls., MN 1949.

Leatherby, Earl C. and John S. Spencer, Jr., Thomas L. Schmidt, Michael Carroll, <u>An Analysis of Minnesota's Fifth Forest Resources Inventory</u>, 1990, USDA For. Serv., North Cen. Exp. Stn., Res. Bul. NC0165, St. Paul, MN 1995.

<u>The Life and Times of Gullford Graham Hartley</u>.

<u>Minnesota's White Pine: Now and for the Future</u>, MN Dept. of Nat. Res., St. Paul, MN, 1996.

Pinchot, Gifford, As cited in <u>The Birth of A Forest: An Account of the Formation of the Chippewa National</u>

<u>Forest</u>, 1898-1907, USDA For. Serv., 1987, 12p.

Rajala, Arthur N., unpublished private papers.

Smith, David M., <u>The Practice of Silviculture</u>, 7th Edition, John Wiley & Sons, Inc., New York, 1986.